ΑΒΡΑΞΑΣ

ABRAXAS

StarGate Publishing House
Las Vegas, NV America
Copyright © July 7, 2020 by THEGOD720
All rights reserved. This publication may not be reproduced, stored in a retrieval system or transmitted, in any form or by any means, electronic, mechanical, photocopying, recording, or otherwise, without the prior permission of the publishers.

TH7S BOOK 7S DED7CATED TO

THE
SUN-D7AL

Content

CHAPTER 7: THE M7ND 5
Chapter 7: The Body 17
Chapter 7: The Land 25
Chapter 7: The 7dea 30
Chapter 7: The Word 56
Chapter 7: The M7th 62
Chapter 7: The Holy 68

Figures

7:) AMPHITHEATRUM SAPIENTIAE AETERNAE – TETRAGRAMMATON TETRAKTYS BY HEINRICH KHUNRATH PG. 1

7:) Naga Tattoo located on the Inner Left Arm of Keenan Booker pg. 57

7:) The Seven Gods of Good Fortune Tosa Mitsuoki (Japanese, 1617–1691) pg. 62

7:) The I Ching Hexagram Number 7 Stands for "Leading" also "The Army & The Troops" pg. 63

7:) Gad, from The Twelve Sons of Jacob: Engraver: Jacques de Gheyn II 1565-1629 The Hague After: Karel van Mander III, Dutch,1608-1670 pg. 65

7:) The Seventh Angel of the Apocalypse Proclaiming the Reign of the Lord circa 1180 pg. 74

7:) A Prostituta da Babilônia - Ponto de Vista Cristão: Colored version of the Whore of Babylon illustration from Martin Luther's 1534 translation of the Bible. Pg. 76

CHAPTER 7: M7ND

The 7 Wild Laws of Success
- 7 Defy the Standard & Stand Out
- 7 Find the Loop Holes
- 7 Study The Winners and Losers before You Enter The Game
- 7 Have High Energy & Intentionally alter Your State of Mind (Euphoria)
- 7 Have a lot of Sex
- 7 Fatten the Pig before You Slaughter
- 7 No Emotional Decision Making/Be Self-Centered

The 7 Forms of Worship
- 7 To Sacrifice / Donation
- 7 Admiration
- 7 Sex
- 7 Dedication
- 7 Slavery
- 7 To Receive or Take Pain
- 7 To do more than asked for / Go Above & Beyond Duty

The 7 Magic Systems
- 7 Words
- 7 Human sacrifice
- 7 Sex
- 7 Music
- 7 Perfection/Beauty
- 7 Unknown Spectacle
- 7 Value

The 7 Wills
- 7 Death/Conclusions/The End
- 7 Chaos
- 7 Life
- 7 Growth
- 7 Attack
- 7 Questions
- 7 Remorse

The 7 Sciences that Divide Human from Animal
- 7 Engineering
- 7 Literature & Reading
- 7 Architecture

- 7 Mathematics
- 7 Chemicals
- 7 Class Systems
- 7 Etiquette

The 7 Acts of Man
- 7 Manipulation
- 7 Violence and/or Killing
- 7 Business and/or Trade
- 7 Competition/Sport
- 7 Create & Complete Goals
- 7 Perversion
- 7 To Possess

The 7 Uses
- 7 Each Other
- 7 Electricity
- 7 Words/Information
- 7 Machinery
- 7 Oil
- 7 Minerals
- 7 Illusion

The 7 Metals
- 7 Gold
- 7 Silver
- 7 Copper
- 7 Platinum
- 7 Lead
- 7 Iron/Steel
- 7 Zinc

The 7 Saints of Entertainment
- 7 St. Martin Lawrence
- 7 St. Vitus
- 7 St. Johns Fire
- 7 St. Cecilia
- 7 St. Genesius of Rome
- 7 St. Catherine of Bologna
- 7 St. Francis de Sales

The 7 Black Madonnas
- 7 Notre Dame d' Afrique
- 7 Good Death
- 7 Black Ethiopian Madonna
- 7 Black Madonna of Czestochowa
- 7 Our Lady of Guadalupe
- 7 Our Lady of Penafrancia
- 7 Theotokos

The 7 Saints of Luck
- 7 St. Corona
- 7 St. Homobonus
- 7 St. Hubertus
- 7 St. Cajetan
- 7 St. Jude The Apostle
- 7 St. Nicholas of Myra
- 7 St. Martin of Tours

The 7 Forces
- 7 Love
- 7 Law
- 7 Maintenance
- 7 Violence
- 7 Courting
- 7 Travel
- 7 Expression / Explanation

The 7 Unifications
- 7 Communication
- 7 Trust / Loyalty
- 7 Sex
- 7 Intoxicants / Liquor
- 7 Food
- 7 Music
- 7 The Atmosphere

The 7 Submissions
- 7 Order
- 7 Your Mate
- 7 Calculation
- 7 Reality

- 7 Intake
- 7 Tests
- 7 Work

The 7 Possibilities
- 7 Being Rich or Poor
- 7 Parenthood and/or marriage
- 7 Robbery
- 7 Failure
- 7 To Be Unliked and/or Lonely
- 7 You Will Be Chosen

The 7 Loves
- 7 Self
- 7 Money
- 7 The Principles of The Opposite Gender
- 7 Consumption
- 7 Euphoria
- 7 The Personal, Individualistic Ritual
- 7 Power/Domination

The 7 Enemies
- 7 Excuses
- 7 Stupidity
- 7 Disease
- 7 Synthetic Foods
- 7 Incompletion
- 7 Separation
- 7 Irresponsibility

The 7 Nevers
- 7 Never Believe or Dream
- 7 Never Attach a Human to your Structure of Happiness
- 7 Never Be Broke
- 7 Never Rely
- 7 Never Stink
- 7 Never Show Your Perversions
- 7 Never Be Late

The 7 Acts of Woman
- 7   Seduction
- 7   Investigation
- 7   Exaggeration
- 7   Denial / Blindness
- 7   To Rely
- 7   Complain
- 7   Expect Slavery and / or Worship

The 7 Gains
- 7   Power
- 7   Authority
- 7   Wealth
- 7   Experiences
- 7   Age
- 7   Knowledge
- 7   Invisibility

The 7 Guarantees
- 7   Life
- 7   Situations
- 7   Hunger
- 7   Pain To Give & Receive
- 7   Lies
- 7   Time
- 7   Change

The 7 Mandatory Responsibilities
- 7   Nature
- 7   Children
- 7   Learn or Develop an Existence
- 7   Your Work and Outcome
- 7   Health
- 7   Anything Possessed
- 7   Your Intelligence

The 7 Important Additions to the Aura
- 7   Sex
- 7   Experiences
- 7   Winning
- 7   Nature

- 7 Power: Financial, Intellectual and Physical Strength
- 7 Travelling
- 7 Medical Feats

The 7 Hates
- 7 Violence
- 7 Anger
- 7 Excommunication / Neglect
- 7 Ignorance
- 7 Pain
- 7 Jealousy
- 7 Genetic Differences

The 7 Desires
- 7 Nourishment
- 7 Water
- 7 Attention
- 7 Gifts / Surprises
- 7 Money
- 7 Nature
- 7 Movement

The 7 Types of Memory Failure
- 7 Transience
- 7 Absent Mindedness
- 7 Blocking
- 7 Misattribution
- 7 Suggestibility
- 7 Bias
- 7 Persistence

The 7 Penances
- 7 Get information of an event immediately after it occurs and it's still fresh in people's minds
- 7 Use a Prioritized Task List
- 7 Take Notes at Important Gatherings
- 7 Record Important Event Daily
- 7 Use neutrally worded questions when soliciting information
- 7 Understand the basis or perspective of the person providing the information.
- 7 Understand and recognize the symptoms of Post Traumatic Syndrome.

The 7 Social Sins
- 7   Wealth without Work
- 7   Pleasure without Conscience
- 7   Knowledge without Character
- 7   Commerce without Morality
- 7   Science without Humanity
- 7   Religion without Sacrifice
- 7   Politics without Principle

The 7 Virtues
- 7   Chastity
- 7   Temperance
- 7   Charity
- 7   Diligence
- 7   Patience
- 7   Kindness
- 7   Humility

The 7 Deadly Sins
- 7   Lust
- 7   Gluttony
- 7   Greed
- 7   Sloth
- 7   Wrath
- 7   Envy
- 7   Pride

The 7 Exploits
- 7   Nudity
- 7   Vanity
- 7   Rage
- 7   Luxury
- 7   The Written Word
- 7   Announcement
- 7   The Stage

The 7 Will Powers
- 7   To Create
- 7   Faith/Hope
- 7   Drive
- 7   Adventure

- 7 Entrapment
- 7 Target
- 7 Possession

The 7 Dirty Words
- 7 Shit
- 7 Piss
- 7 Fuck
- 7 Cunt
- 7 Cocksucker
- 7 Motherfucker
- 7 Tits

The 7 Feminine Desires
- 7 Beauty
- 7 To be sought & manipulated
- 7 For you to not know
- 7 For you to not see
- 7 All forms of pain
- 7 To sleep
- 7 To be heard and not to be heard

The 7 Emotions of Adam & Eve After The Garden of Eden
- 7 Confusion
- 7 Depression
- 7 Stress
- 7 Neglect/Depravation
- 7 Anger
- 7 Remorse
- 7 Detachment

The 7 Devil Attacks
- 7 Love
- 7 Laughter
- 7 Liquor
- 7 Illusion
- 7 Omitting & Emitting
- 7 Addiction
- 7 Spontaneous Acts

The 7 Graces
- 7 Prophecy
- 7 Assistance
- 7 Instruction
- 7 Encouragement
- 7 Generosity
- 7 Guidance
- 7 Compassion

The 7 Watcher Angels
- 7 Uriel
- 7 Raphael
- 7 Raguel
- 7 Michael
- 7 Sarakiel
- 7 Gabriel
- 7 Phanuel

The 7 Joys of The Virgin
- 7 The Annunciation
- 7 The Nativity of Jesus
- 7 The Adoration of The Magi
- 7 The Resurrection of Christ
- 7 The Ascension of Christ to Heaven
- 7 The Pentecost
- 7 The Coronation of The Virgin in Heaven

The 7 Gods
- 7 Aton
- 7 YHWH
- 7 Buddah
- 7 Allah
- 7 Quetzalcoatl
- 7 Anansi
- 7 Thor

The 7 Mysteries
- 7 OuterSpace & The Sol
- 7 Time & Existence
- 7 Love
- 7 The Known Unknowns

- 7   The Toxicity of The Human Body and The Chemistry of All Things
- 7   The Author of Metaphysics & Astrology
- 7   Death & The Afterlife

The 7 Invisible Beings
- 7   Fallen Angels
- 7   Djinns
- 7   Death
- 7   The Devil & Demons
- 7   Gremlins
- 7   Saints
- 7   The Entities that Live in A Word

The 7 Codex's
- 7   All Papyrus, Hieroglyphics and All Kemetan Walls
- 7   Codex Vaticanus
- 7   Codex Sinaiticus
- 7   Codex Alexandrinus
- 7   Codex Ephraemi Rescriptus
- 7   Codex Gigas
- 7   The Dresden Codex

The 7 Bibles
- 7   King James Bible
- 7   The Apocrypha (Missing Books of The Bible)
- 7   The Black Man's Bible
- 7   The Torah
- 7   The Quran
- 7   Gutenberg Bible
- 7   The Talmud

The 7 Heretical Groups
- 7   Luciferians
- 7   The Brothers of Friendship
- 7   Albigensis
- 7   Waldensians
- 7   Catharists
- 7   Illuminati

The 7 Executioners of Law
- 7   The Law
- 7   The Executioner
- 7   The Rope
- 7   Karma
- 7   The Chopping Block
- 7   Poison
- 7   Mysticism

The 7 Sigil Systems
- 7   Enochian Magic (Angel Communication)
- 7   VooDoo
- 7   The Goetia
- 7   Celtic
- 7   The Crowley Systems
- 7   Hieroglyphics
- 7   Logos

The 7 Warning Signs
- 7   Smoke
- 7   Screams
- 7   Alteration of the Original condition of anything
- 7   Hand Signals
- 7   Blood
- 7   Tears
- 7   Sound

The 7 Laws of Attraction
- 7   Your Habits
- 7   Your Overall Bodily Intake that's Visions & Food
- 7   The Opposites
- 7   Religion
- 7   Similar Experiences
- 7   Likes & Favoritism
- 7   Genetics / Natural Selection / Family

The 7 Bodies of The Human
- 7   Skin
- 7   Bones
- 7   Muscles
- 7   Nerves & Brain

- 7 Aura (Electricity)
- 7 Hair
- 7 Name

The 7 Solitudes
- 7 Reading / Writing
- 7 Meditation
- 7 Hunting / Fishing
- 7 The Woods / Ocean / Air
- 7 Defecating
- 7 Sleep
- 7 Jail

The 7 Messiahs
- 7 Emmanuel
- 7 Muhammad
- 7 Enoch
- 7 Elijah / Elias
- 7 Yeshuah
- 7 Buddha
- 7 Melchezideck

The 7 Projectiles
- 7 Bow & Arrow
- 7 Sling Shot
- 7 Catapult
- 7 Firearm
- 7 Rifle
- 7 Small Bombs (Grenade)
- 7 Dynamite

The 7 Lady Parts
- 7 Tits
- 7 Toes
- 7 Legs
- 7 Ass
- 7 Lips
- 7 Eyes
- 7 Hands

The 7 Gangstas
- 7 Any Organization that Uses Violence as a Force
- 7 Gangsta Disciple
- 7 Any Business Man
- 7 Soldiers / Platoon
- 7 The Police
- 7 The Orders
- 7 Crip & Blood Sets with Gangsta attached to the Set Name

The 7 Vices
- 7 Advice
- 7 Vice President
- 7 Victory (Vice Story)
- 7 Vicariousness
- 7 Victim (Vice Time)
- 7 Vice Lord
- 7 Vice Grip

The 7 Sacrifices
- 7 Animals
- 7 Children or mate
- 7 Sex
- 7 Relationships
- 7 Material Possessions
- 7 Money
- 7 Comfort / Time

Chapter 7: Body

The 7 Physical Enhancements
- 7 Water
- 7 B12
- 7 Exercise
- 7 Walking
- 7 Marijuana / Ergot
- 7 Sex
- 7 Acception

The 7 Modern Day Plagues
- 7 STD's & AIDS
- 7 Cancer
- 7 Imagery

- 7   Synthetic Chemicals
- 7   Influence
- 7   Depravation
- 7   Anything Contagious

The 7 Ology's of Man
- 7   Astrology
- 7   Biology
- 7   Ecology
- 7   Zoology
- 7   Psychology
- 7   Anthropology
- 7   Sociology

The 7 Chemicals of Human
- 7   Testosterone
- 7   Estrogen
- 7   Oxygen
- 7   Carbon/Melanin
- 7   Cancer Cells
- 7   Nitrogen
- 7   Phosphorus

The 7 Ancient Tongues
- 7   Sanskrit
- 7   MTU NTR
- 7   Latin
- 7   Greek
- 7   Hebrew
- 7   The Cave Mans Grunts
- 7   Buntu

The 7 Needs of Man
- 7   Fire & Nature this includes Animals
- 7   Numbers
- 7   Written word
- 7   Woman
- 7   Silence
- 7   Focus
- 7   Water

The 7 Technologies
- 7 The Human Nervous system
- 7 Electricity
- 7 The Internet
- 7 Smelting
- 7 The Mill (Water)
- 7 Aero-Dynamics
- 7 Frequency

The 7 Ethers
- 7 Skin
- 7 Hair
- 7 Bone Marrow
- 7 Fully Ethereal (Gas)
- 7 Semi-Ethereal (Liquid)
- 7 Trace Amount (Solid)
- 7 Atmosphere

The 7 Eyes
- 7 Red
- 7 Black
- 7 Yellow
- 7 All Seeing
- 7 Blind
- 7 Evil Eye
- 7 Third

The 7 Tongues
- 7 Gold
- 7 Silver
- 7 Slit
- 7 Black
- 7 English/Spanish
- 7 Judgment
- 7 Tasting

The 7 Dependencies
- 7 Sun / Light
- 7 Water
- 7 Elders
- 7 Written Word

- 7 Clarity
- 7 Agreeance
- 7 Children

The 7 Candles
- 7 Left Eye
- 7 Right Eye
- 7 Left Ear
- 7 Right Ear
- 7 Left Nostril
- 7 Right Nostril
- 7 The Mouth

The 7 Corporal Works of Mercy
- 7 To feed The Hungry
- 7 To give water to the Thirsty
- 7 To clothe The Naked
- 7 To shelter The Homeless
- 7 To visit The Sick
- 7 To Visit the imprisoned or Ransom the Captive
- 7 To bury The Dead

To 7 Spiritual Works of Mercy
- 7 To Instruct the Ignorant
- 7 To Counsel the Doubtful
- 7 To Admonish the Sinners
- 7 To Bear Patiently those Who Wrong Us.
- 7 To Forgive Offenses
- 7 To Comfort the Afflicted.
- 7 To Pray for The Living and The Dead

The 7 Chakras
- 7 Crown
- 7 Third Eye
- 7 Throat
- 7 Heart
- 7 Naval
- 7 Sexual Organs
- 7 Base of Spine

The 7 Monster Ingredients
- 7   Violence
- 7   Sexual Dominance
- 7   Risk Taking & Achievements
- 7   Survival of Harsh Conditions
- 7   Unlimited Money
- 7   Advanced Intelligence
- 7   Not Needing

The 7 Types of Caveman
- 7   Cro-Magnon
- 7   Java Man
- 7   Neanderthal
- 7   Homo-Erectus
- 7   Homo-Sapien Sapien
- 7   The Caveman
- 7   Homo Habilis

The 7 Self Defenses
- 7   Avoidance
- 7   Hand to Hand Combat
- 7   Financial
- 7   Loved Ones
- 7   The Courageous Stranger
- 7   Attack First
- 7   Weaponry

The 7 Euphoria's
- 7   Alcohol
- 7   Sex
- 7   Opium
- 7   Marijuana/Tobacco
- 7   Cocaine
- 7   Chemicals
- 7   Food

The 7 Chaos's
- 7   Nature \ Weather
- 7   Thinking
- 7   War
- 7   The Opposite Gender

- 7 Euphoria
- 7 Gaming/Gambling
- 7 Attempting to Control or Maintenance of a Thing

The 7 Vices of Success
- 7 Alcohol
- 7 No Sleep
- 7 Stress
- 7 A lot of Sex or No Sex
- 7 Sweat
- 7 The Unseen Hand
- 7 Cursing

The 7 Invisible Addictions
- 7 Sugar
- 7 Coffee
- 7 Cheese
- 7 Bread
- 7 Seeking Attention
- 7 Money
- 7 Music

The 7 Visible Addictions
- 7 Smoking
- 7 Food/Obesity
- 7 Beauty
- 7 Technology
- 7 Alcohol
- 7 Business/Work
- 7 Travelling

The 7 Alcohols
- 7 Scotch/Whiskey
- 7 Cognac
- 7 Bourbon
- 7 Wine
- 7 Beer
- 7 Vodka/Moonshine
- 7 Tequila

The 7 Invisible Demands of Royals
- 7 Honor
- 7 Respect
- 7 Loyalty
- 7 Trustworthiness
- 7 Reliance
- 7 Protection
- 7 Secrets

The 7 Invisible Beauties
- 7 Prestige
- 7 Glamour
- 7 Fame
- 7 Intelligence
- 7 Stability
- 7 Survival
- 7 Deception / Illusion

The 7 Self Defeats
- 7 Pride
- 7 Lies
- 7 Lack of Seriousness
- 7 Not Impeding
- 7 Creating Excuses
- 7 Fear
- 7 Prior Failure

The 7 Maturities
- 7 Walking / Talking
- 7 Immoral Acts
- 7 Violence
- 7 Puberty
- 7 Coercing & Chasing
- 7 Sex
- 7 Money

The 7 Unspeakable Acts
- 7 Homosexuality
- 7 Bestiality
- 7 Coprophilia
- 7 Necrophilia

- 7   Rape
- 7   Sex with Children (Pederasty)
- 7   Sex with Dolls

The 7 Hellish Entities
- 7   The Werewolf
- 7   The Undead
- 7   Vampire
- 7   Fiend
- 7   Witch
- 7   Poltergeist
- 7   Devil

The 7 Stages of Humans
- 7   Embryo
- 7   Infant
- 7   Child
- 7   Teenager
- 7   Pre-Adult
- 7   Mother / Father
- 7   Elderly

The 7 Rulers of Society
- 7   Religion
- 7   Words/Media
- 7   Government
- 7   Education
- 7   Economy
- 7   Family
- 7   Celebrations/Arts

The 7 Types of Women
- 7   Voluptuous/Amazon
- 7   Ugly
- 7   Stern
- 7   Motherly/Mammy
- 7   Virgin, Mother Mary & Mary Magdalene
- 7   Goddess/Beautiful
- 7   Jealous

Chapter 7: The Land

The 7 Elements
- 7 Water
- 7 Light
- 7 Fire
- 7 Air
- 7 Mineral
- 7 The Spheres
- 7 Time

The 7 Ravagers
- 7 The Lion
- 7 Shark
- 7 Piranha
- 7 The Alligator
- 7 Hyena
- 7 The Wolf
- 7 The Eagle

The 7 Spheres
- 7 Exosphere
- 7 Thermosphere
- 7 Mesosphere
- 7 Stratosphere
- 7 Troposphere
- 7 Wordsphere
- 7 Ethersphere

The 7 Thrones
- 7 Books
- 7 The Internet
- 7 Money
- 7 Law
- 7 Land/Vegetation
- 7 The Air
- 7 Water

The 7 Celestial Objects seen by The Human Eye
- 7 Sun
- 7 Moon

- 7 Mars
- 7 Mercury
- 7 Jupiter
- 7 Venus
- 7 Saturn

The 7 Wonders of The Ancient World
- 7 Great Pyramid of Giza
- 7 Hanging Gardens of Babylon
- 7 Temple of Artemis at Ephesus
- 7 Statue of Zeus at Olympia
- 7 Mausoleum at Halicarnassus
- 7 Colossus of Rhodes
- 7 Lighthouse of Alexandria

The 7 Colors of The Rainbow
- 7 Red
- 7 Orange
- 7 Yellow
- 7 Green
- 7 Blue
- 7 Indigo
- 7 Violet

The 7 Continents
- 7 Africa
- 7 Antarctica
- 7 Asia
- 7 Europe
- 7 North America
- 7 Australia
- 7 South America

The 7 Days of The Week
- 7 Sunday
- 7 Monday
- 7 Tuesday
- 7 Wednesday
- 7 Thursday
- 7 Friday
- 7 Saturday

The 7 Seas
- 7   Arctic Ocean
- 7   North Atlantic Ocean
- 7   South Atlantic Ocean
- 7   Indian Ocean
- 7   North Pacific Ocean
- 7   South Pacific Ocean
- 7   The Antarctic Ocean

The 7 Ancient Civilizations
- 7   Kemet/Egypt
- 7   Greece
- 7   Babylonia/Sumeria
- 7   Maya
- 7   Phoenicia
- 7   Inca
- 7   Rome

The 7 Ways of Astrology
- 7   The Animals Physical, Sexual & Habitual Operation in Nature
- 7   The Planet that Rules the Sign
- 7   Astro-Biology
- 7   Numbers
- 7   Archetypes / Stereotypes & Psychological / Societal Influence
- 7   Repetitive Research
- 7   The other 76 signs within & without our solar system

The 7 Precious Stones
- 7   Diamond
- 7   Sapphire
- 7   Ruby
- 7   Emerald
- 7   Peridot
- 7   Tanzanite
- 7   Lapis Lazuli

The 7 Nothings
- 7   Space
- 7   The Canvas
- 7   An Instrument with No Human

- 7 Still Born
- 7 A Human with No Name
- 7 A Human with no Achievements
- 7 Anything without Energy Source

The 7 Colors of Fire
- 7 Red
- 7 Orange
- 7 Green
- 7 Blue
- 7 White
- 7 Black
- 7 Purple

The 7 Frequencies
- 7 Cellular
- 7 Color
- 7 Sound
- 7 Solar
- 7 Vibration
- 7 Cosmo
- 7 Humans Individually and Collectively

The 7 Alchemical Ingredients
- 7 Astrology
- 7 Earth (Herbs & Oil)
- 7 Air (Mysticism / Angles & Devils)
- 7 Human Energy (Essence / Force / Will Power)
- 7 Physick (Body Parts Human & Animal)
- 7 Signs / Sigils / Symbols / Words & Numbers
- 7 Principles of Merging

The 7 Geographical Concepts
- 7 Place
- 7 Space
- 7 Environment
- 7 Interconnection
- 7 Sustainability
- 7 Scale
- 7 Change

The 7 Stars of The Big Dipper
- 7   Dubhe
- 7   Merak
- 7   Phecda
- 7   Megrez
- 7   Alioth
- 7   Mizar
- 7   Alkaid

The 7 Most Remote Locations on Earth
- 7   Tristan de Cunha
- 7   Avenue of the Baobabs
- 7   Kerguelen Islands
- 7   Ittoqqortoormiit, Greenland
- 7   Devon Island
- 7   Changtang, Tibet
- 7   McMurdo Station, Antartica

The 7 Natural Land Biomes
- 7   Tropical Rainforests
- 7   Temperate Forests
- 7   Deserts
- 7   Tundra
- 7   Taiga
- 7   Grasslands
- 7   Savana

The 7 Times
- 7   Personal
- 7   The Day
- 7   The Week
- 7   The Year
- 7   The Seasons
- 7   The Solar System
- 7   Chaos

The 7 Laws of The Universe
- 7   Law of Vibration
- 7   Law of Relativity
- 7   Law of Cause and Effect
- 7   Law of Polarity

- 7 Law of Gestation
- 7 Law of Rhythm
- 7 Law of Gestation

The 7 Ancient Wonders of China
- 7 Qin Shi Huangs Mausoleum The Terracotta Army
- 7 The Great Wall of China
- 7 The Forbidden City
- 7 The Hangzhou Beijing Canal
- 7 Dujiangyan Irrigation System
- 7 The Sanxingdui and Jinsha Relics
- 7 The Dali Pagodas

The 7 Treasures of Buddhism
- 7 Gold
- 7 Silver
- 7 Pearls
- 7 Lapis Lazuli
- 7 Rock Crystal
- 7 Amber
- 7 Cornelian

The 7 Devils are peaks in Idaho in the Hells Canyon wilderness.
The 7 Sisters of The Pleiades Star System
The 7 Colored Earth is Located in Mauritius
The 7 Magic Mountains of Las Vegas, Nevada
The 777 Tower is Located in Los Angeles, California.

Chapter 7: The 7dea

&

The Corona Plague Philosophy

- 777 Take Care of Dumb Asses and Be a Hamster in a Wheel.
- 777 Understand What Value is Before You Act like You Are Valuable.
- 777 To Ignore Is to Be Ignorant.
- 777 Loneliness Settles in The Sol, Love Only settles in The Heart.
- 777 The Woman's Energy Is Always Needed.
- 777 Expect Nothing from No One.
- 777 The Lone Wolf is Not Allowed to Believe in Friends & Only in Gaining

- 777   Shit, was Always Real, You was just Living in Fakeness.
- 777   A Small Mind Thinks What it Sees is All that's Going On.
- 777   If You Know Nothing about Plague, Then Don't Run your Plaque Mouth.
- 777   Always Remember Animals Don't Understand Magic, It is a Human Art.
- 777   Once You Kill Masculinity, You have Invited The Devil.
- 777   Keep The Yosemite Sam on the Hip And The Elmer Fudd in the House.
- 777   You live in Western Culture which is White Thought If You Don't Know their History, You Don't Know What You're Doing or Saying.
- 777   Witches hate Fairies They'll Never be in the same Room Even on Cartoons
- 777   Reality can Only Be Altered By Words.
- 777   All Fantasies Have an Expiration Date.
- 777   A Man's Words Is a Woman's Illusion.
- 777   The funny thing about insanity is. A Person can't tell when they are Insane.
- 777   Never take an Opinion From a Dollar Menu Eater.
- 777   To Be Aligned With Superiority Is to Ensure your Security.
- 777   Toxicity begins with The Thought As Acid controls Your Body.
- 777   Move the Invisible or Hope for Nothing.
- 777   Sacrifices Are Always Compensated for.
- 777   Submission Is Always Honored.
- 777   Invite Challenges And Inculcate Power.
- 777   The Possessive Woman Attacks Sexually.
- 777   Prepare your Nose for Stronger Scents.
- 777   It's funny watching people talk about shit they know nothing about.
- 777   Your Lack of Focus Is your Guaranteed Failure.
- 777   If you haven't Studied or Practiced Medical, Your Opinion on the Matters of Plague are Worthless as is your Brain.
- 777   You Chose the Road of The Retard and Consequences are Imminent.
- 777   The Plague Is Spiritual Not Microscopic.
- 777   Fall in Love with Death And Be Undefeatable.
- 777   Be Selfless In Your Way.
- 777   You are Nothing to No One Until You Have Done something for Man Kind.
- 777   Loose Your Pride And Survive.
- 777   Your Distribution of Love Balances The Health of Your Existence.
- 777   Only the God Pan Understands Panic & Pandemonium.
- 777   Secrets Weight Down Your Sol.
- 777   Only stay Loyal to Royals Because The Rest are Depressed from Success.
- 777   All Women are Potential Baits in the Time of Plague.
- 777   All Adults Will have Tricks up their Sleeve during Times of Plague.
- 777   Let No Child Be Lost Or Roam Free In the Time of Plague.
- 777   Always remember Indigenous people are not Serious Individuals.
- 777   Cell Phones have Killed more Relationships than Cheating.
- 777   Those who get Hype Are another Man's Puppet.

- 777 Allow Societal Influence and have No Sol.
- 777 Heal your Depression by getting Sexually Worshipped.
- 777 Seriousness is the Gasoline to Success.
- 777 Your Boldness Predicates your Distance.
- 777 Those who Read don't have to Listen To Those Who Don't Read
- 777 Your Confusion Is another's Amusement.
- 777 Spider Webbed minds Catch Nothing.
- 777 The Empty Seductress Online fulfills Graves.
- 777 You Can Only Dream with Your Eyes Closed.
- 777 Love is Stronger Than Pride But both are Invisible.
- 777 Being Excited Is to X the Site. The Destination on a Treasure Map The Targeted Center.
- 777 The Innocent Are In No Sense.
- 777 Protect, Reflect and Deflect Etcetera.
- 777 You Repel Love & Money with the Lack of Communication.
- 777 The Woman is The Fruit & All Her Parts better Smell Like The Garden of Eden.
- 777 To Respond Is to be Responsible.
- 777 To Be Free for a Woman is to let a Woman Be Free.
- 777 When People state "It's to good to be true" It usually isn't. Their mind is just wired to only comprehend misery and lies.
- 777 I'll Teach You Freedom.
- 777 When Intelligence becomes your addiction, OVERDOSE MY FRIEND
- 777 There's no such thing as an alpha woman they all bend over
- 777 In order to provide, you spend money. But not with a disagreeable woman who uses the words "no" and "don't".
- 777 Quick Decisions are based on Animal impulse or Mathematical absolution.
- 777 The word "probably" acts like a virus in the female mind.
- 777 The highway of intelligence is built on a combination of the plants of euphoria and sex.
- 777 A brain that glitches Is unsuccessful.
- 777 The male who is not an entrepreneur has nothing to lead.
- 777 Ladies usually don't make things happen. They are the happening that is made.
- 777 Social Media Has Destroyed at Least 10,000 inventions for the next century.
- 777 The quick woman wins and gets to keep.
- 777 The mind has no limitation.
- 777 Ladies: Sex is now therapy, Not a bait for slavery.
- 777 To let the unknown rule is to be a waiting fool.
- 777 Copying is the mind of the robot whether that be flesh or steel.
- 777 If the sun was as slow as the modern day response there would be no growth.

- 777 Enjoy Stench as much as the sweet scents and become God.
- 777 During pregnancy a woman's lower body is on earth her upper body is in outer space.
- 777 You are only a brain, eyes and a nervous system. The rest is an outfit.
- 777 A Complaint is Proof of Inadequacy for an Animal cannot Complain.
- 777 Underestimate your enemies and Rot in your slavery
- 777 The walls you put in front of you are blocks in the mind and knots on the nerves
- 777 Enjoy your position and salivate at the mouth for the next level
- 777 Superiority and Inferiority are concepts that only the inferior won't accept
- 777 Your ignorance Will be your eulogy.
- 777 Always abandon the little girl who chooses not.
- 777 Success gives a form of alpha male allowance. All those who achieve it are not alpha males.
- 777 From Ants to Atom Bombs You are on a planet of killers.
- 777 The Brain that doesn't work in a process and procedure form is actually a dog chasing its tail.
- 777 It takes 2 years of living with someone to truly know who they are.
- 777 Dating is child's play, Get to the point Were adults and got shit to do.
- 777 Ladies: seek the inexperienced male for emotional safety and produce the weak child.
- 777 Emotions destroy more then they create.
- 777 In the wild: weakness is another's meal.
- 777 After 30 a woman can no longer be bashful She must Hunt Everything.
- 777 Those who dig find Gold or Bones.
- 777 Mimic & copy the stranger, Is following the path of the unknown.
- 777 Be indecisive and Prove your worthlessness.
- 777 The abuse women enjoy during sex was encoded in them from everyday life of human existence over 10,000 years ago.
- 777 Sex is more of a biological maintenance Then it is to fulfill the emotion.
- 777 Prepare for blood When in a vagabonds Labyrinth.
- 777 Seek what you can attain & possess, To not seek is Peace in Rest.
- 777 To Love again and again, is tiresome Work.
- 777 An Incomplete Mind Will Leave One Abandoned.
- 777 Every woman's body has sugar content her scent & taste is sweet naturally.
- 777 The Woman that keeps a garden understands time
- 777 The Woman that Runs Home, Makes Flowers Blossom
- 777 Believe in Revenge and Make The Dead Smile
- 777 Pain is the cup of the beggar
- 777 Ensure your superiority by the others lack
- 777 Release Blood And Feel Peace
- 777 She is filled with Naught & Vice
- 777 If you are not the authority do not test

- 777 Learn Internal and be Eternal, Enjoy the External and Parish in the Inferno
- 777 Money and Orgasm Is the way of the human
- 777 Look Down and Know that ye are above
- 777 Communication is a tennis match
- 777 Never let sympathy be your reason for attraction
- 777 In all your breathing Let the dead breathe
- 777 Enforce your illusions and gain nothing
- 777 Act the Role and Achieve the goal
- 777 Humiliate yourself And destroy the devils pride
- 777 Starving is the first stage of Winning
- 777 Walk the fires of hell and come out the sharpest sword
- 777 There is no age to blood therefore you are age old
- 777 Hunt and Be quick with your gatherings
- 777 The Dark Arts And The Dark Acts Are 2 Different Things
- 777 Ravage the woman and she will know your capability of security
- 777 Human and animal Will never be separated
- 777 Good is Only the Apology of Evil
- 777 All Things are Taken
- 777 To be Invisible is the Goal
- 777 You become what you fight
- 777 To Publish is to Embed in the Atmosphere
- 777 Your Perversion is Your Highway of Creation from the Galaxy
- 777 A Problem is something to do
- 777 To be Scared is To be Prepared
- 777 The Allowance of Vulnerability is The Releasing of Sol Congestion
- 777 Break all Fears.
- 777 Conquer at Will, Ahoy!
- 777 Submit To nothing
- 777 A woman's breast need as much attention as her coon coon
- 777 Congestion creates illusions, therefore big girls are viewed as treasure chests
- 777 A woman's smothering love is the investment of Riches
- 777 You are on Earth which is essentially Kicked Out of Heaven
- 777 The Pretty Beggar Wins
- 777 Lively & Bright
- 777 A Domesticated Pig released to the Wild in 3 months will return to a Boar with tusks, the moral of the story is You can't change anybody
- 777 Stay Loyal to stupidity and stagnate your life
- 777 A woman's toes are the same as the roots of the plant
- 777 The Gelatin Baby Fat of the Woman Is the matter of Life
- 777 Speak to the Vagina And your voice is heard In Outer Space
- 777 Nothing is Complete
- 777 A No Body Is a Body with no Head. They are only used for their mind.

- 777 Some Words have over a Million Sols in them
- 777 Respect is a Magic System
- 777 To be an Alpha Male is found in Experience and Conquering the Invisible and Women
- 777 Your intelligence Is Your responsibility
- 777 You must be still to grow as it is the same when you decay
- 777 Those who seek attention Have no Mirror
- 777 To Pretend Is to Blend and Have No End
- 777 The Little Girl seeks Love & The Woman Fears It
- 777 You have No Art If you have No Passion & you have No Passion If you have No Survival
- 777 No One Knows What they are Born for until The Deed is Done
- 777 The animal mind relies only on the tangible
- 777 You're alive, therefore you are experiencing a death penalty right now
- 777 To be simple is to not be involved in activity that does not have gain
- 777 To Dream and Survive is the Way of the Woman
- 777 The mind is a computer and seriousness is a software everybody's mind doesn't have
- 777 A liars heart and throat chakra are not connected
- 777 The human body is built for euphoria Of all kinds
- 777 The flesh and the mind have 2 different ages
- 777 Momentary thinking is the religion of the Vagabond
- 777 The Rules of Engagement are the Laws of War
- 777 Judgment is Limitation As Freedom is Vulnerability
- 777 Deprivation is the Fuel to Conquer
- 777 Be Extreme And Get the Answer
- 777 Fear Intelligence And Prove your stupidity
- 777 Be Infatuated Or Possess Nothing
- 777 Reach 4 The Phenomenal My Nigga Snatch Sols at Will
- 777 There is no ball and chain greater than the mind and nerves
- 777 Those who want to be chased, must first have no chains and baggage
- 777 The Heart is Now a Piece of Art at a Museum and Love, The Red Velvet Rope in Front
- 777 Only True Artists can Express Any Emotion With No Shame
- 777 Hate is Useless
- 777 People will get mad at you for being Self sufficient
- 777 Understand The Cave Man Was The First Artist
- 777 Women are The True Source of Art
- 777 Intoxication & Role Play Allow More Mental Expansion than Thinking
- 777 The Eyes Watch As The Mind Steals
- 777 Force is the Battery of Desire as Manipulation is its Security
- 777 No surgery can be done on the spirit of the Heart
- 777 People Act like they want to be in your life Until there's no more Scenes

- 777 To Be Detailed Is To Be De-Tailed To Not Think in Animal Form
- 777 When You See No Value You Lose All Desire
- 777 Lose All Faith & Gain Freedom
- 777 Stupid people think smart people are the devil and smart people think stupid people are the devil Play Ball
- 777 Think what you want about me I've made money every day during the plague.... doing nothing
- 777 Deny Making Love And Prove Your Evil
- 777 You Only Tease when you're a child
- 777 You Must Hunt for Love
- 777 Fear Your Own Tears
- 777 You Never really break her. You break the traumas she thought was supposed to be a part of her character
- 777 The mind is not the brain, the heart is not the sol, kiss her on her forehead until she feels it in her toes
- 777 Blind yourself and be another man's food
- 777 Obedience is not a thing you force a woman to do. It's just in some girl's hearts, usually the fairies.
- 777 Stay away from people who can't make quick decisions. It's usually because they're inexperienced
- 777 We'll never know if this disease shit is real
- 777 Let The Imagination be the Playground for the woman & child As Reality is the Battlefield of Men
- 777 2 types of thinking for humans: Animal Impulse Or Human Strategy
- 777 A high wired person Is as worthless as the confused brain that operates them
- 777 I study Human Behavior so I see people's true colors from the jump. Didn't have to wait for a Plague.
- 777 Anything You Post You Promote, Be Smart.
- 777 Keep The Mind Busy With Work & Women & See No Misery
- 777 It's just Numbers on a Screen and Low Life Dumbasses online seeking attention posting lies
- 777 Adults who seek fun are usually running from traumas of the mind and responsibilities of their time
- 777 Work & Gain stress Fuck & Relieve stress Repeat & Stay sane.
- 777 Art is a Responsibility for Aliens, Gods & Angels, Not Mimicing Fools
- 777 If your Art was Designed for Income You Have Taught Man-Kind Nothing
- 777 Only the Gorgeous, Gorge
- 777 All Preparation is Psychological
- 777 Humans are Designed to Seek Euphoria. So We Make Love in Times of Peril.
- 777 Don't Expect to be with a Man that has Survival skills. When you aint got Obedient skills

- 777 Comply Or Complicate You Decide
- 777 The Fear of The Plague Is just as Bad As The Plague
- 777 Your Loved ones rather see your face last before they go. Rest is better than Misery
- 777 Ignore the woman's passivity
- 777 Those who aren't Serious now Will be insane vagabonds later
- 777 Those who are oblivious Are dangerous
- 777 To Want & To Hunt
- 777 Masculinity is back Blow the dust off your oven mittens ladies.
- 777 No Conspiracy Theorists Provides A Solution
- 777 Everything & Everyone Is Optional
- 777 I'm a Business Man So Cooperation & Order Rules over Love & Freedom
- 777 Lack of Solidarity Provides Victimization
- 777 When you Have No Environmental Intelligence, You Perceive No Value
- 777 Defiance Will Not Allow You to Survive or Succeed.
- 777 Childish Uneducated Adults are Dangerous.
- 777 There is a Chain of Command as there is A Chain of Events.
- 777 Avoid the Woman's Tears in the Time of Peril.
- 777 Seek your Attention Now, When There are Ghosts amongst You.
- 777 The Woman's Obedience Will Heal the Coronavirus.
- 777 Country Is Really Cunt-try.
- 777 There is Nothing Without Man Power.
- 777 Be a Slave And Be Free from Responsibility which is Never Maturing.
- 777 Positivity & Negativity is Balanced upon Perception.
- 777 The Home is the Way of the Slave as Travelling is the Way of the Animal.
- 777 Anything can Be Philosophized upon But Everything is Not Philosophy.
- 777 What is an artist without another's eyes, ears, heart and sol They need not think
- 777 Every Humans Mind begins as a Witches Pot
- 777 Those who run will need their knees For other things
- 777 Vulnerability is Not Wise As an Adult
- 777 To be attached Is to be Responsible
- 777 Fame is Not Money nor is it Important
- 777 To Survive Off of your Art is Not the Art of Survival
- 777 Being born an Artist and Forcing yourself to Attain Fame are 2 different things.
- 777 When this is all over I hope people realize how much of a dumbass they are and stop allowing outside influences
- 777 To Lie is to consider ones emotions and care about their feelings
- 777 Place yourself in the human sol and be admired by all
- 777 Fame is invisible and is attained by human belief
- 777 An artist's mind Is a woman's dream
- 777 The woman is sought for pleasantness Which is pure when not purchased

- 777 Stand your ground as if in concrete to your knees
- 777 A sentence is a conviction from one sol applied to another. Watch what one says To you
- 777 It is better to possess and keep Then to beg and weep
- 777 Loneliness settles in The Sol Love only settles in The Heart
- 777 The Last Generation raised us to be their slaves. Not to be Successful.
- 777 Rather be Solo Then Listen to some Unachievers Mouth
- 777 Generation X: the only generation that followed the ways of its children.
- 777 If you don't read nonfiction books You're fucking retarded And there's no way around this No shortcuts
- 777 Your mind is all you truly have
- 777 Being born an Artist and Forcing yourself to Attain Fame are 2 different things.
- 777 Anything can be philosophized upon But everything is not Philosophy
- 777 She Flies on The Goat Backwards
- 777 As Diamonds & Gold Come from inside the Dirt Only the Dead Need to Drape themselves with such
- 777 Inbox Is another word for Coochie
- 777 Harry Potter Is another word for Coochie
- 777 Nobodies Mind is Prepared for This
- 777 I Feel The Black Madonna's Heart Pulsate With Worry
- 777 Women: Your Ladiness is your Magic and your Power. Tattoos Destroy your Quality
- 777 Lack of Solidarity Provides Victimization
- 777 I'm a Business Man So Cooperation & Order Rules over Love & Freedom
- 777 If you stayed attached to any form of media for the past 20 years. You think like a woman.
- 777 She wants to "Go Out" all the time. When the household she grew up in was traumatic.
- 777 That relationship shit is overrated. Only needed when you're broke.
- 777 Does Bleach kill the woman's desire to be territorial? Asking for a friend
- 777 Teases Don't Work with a Lion Fuck around and get Ravaged & Devoured
- 777 I Love being Serious
- 777 The Cave Man Act Has been Passed
- 777 I'm so glad I wasn't attached to useless shit no way
- 777 Quarantine & Play with your Jelly Bean
- 777 Live in the Moment & Only Live for a Moment Legends Live Forever
- 777 Be Aggressive
- 777 Complete your Missions
- 777 To be for real I don't play video games Because I think were already in one
- 777 It takes a lot of experiences, a lot of reading and acception with reality in order to think clear and stay sane

- 777 Blind yourself and be another man's food
- 777 Understand Ladies Your Future is More Important than Your Mouth
- 777 You Must Hunt for Love
- 777 The God Pan doesn't Panic
- 777 You Only Tease when you're a child
- 777 Deny Making Love And Prove Your Evil
- 777 You've watched so many movies. You can't divide reality from falsehood. Blame yourself.
- 777 I'm too grown, Mature and paid To chase you
- 777 Stupid people think smart people are the devil and smart people think stupid people are the devil PLAY BALL
- 777 When You See No Value You Lose All Desire
- 777 Revolutionary women have angry coon coon
- 777 Don't waste money Don't waste time
- 777 Real Men have too many responsibilities to be worried about fun.
- 777 1 reason I write books is because I've learned, healing another's issues is a waste of time and non-monetary
- 777 Women want me to think small & about them. The world is my responsibility, be a queen to that or a slave.
- 777 Stay away from people who think they are right But their childhood is filled with traumatic experiences They are very confused
- 777 The Speculation of a Dumbass is the Lack of Investigation of a Jackass
- 777 You don't have depression you have dumbassitis
- 777 You don't have anxiety you have stupidifida
- 777 Phone = Phony Fame Fake Fate All the same word
- 777 Her main Ingredient Was always Obedience
- 777 It is better to be seductive, then destructive.
- 777 You can't make the feet of a bum, tread a royal path.
- 777 Monogamy will be destroyed
- 777 Success requires more books than dreams
- 777 The world will go back to normal and the woman will bake and maintain her home as a help meet and no leader
- 777 I see Hecate and Diana want War. It will end in a 3some to their exhaustion and expense.
- 777 Your wounds heal on their own.
- 777 The Only Thing in Existence that Guarantees Sound Mental Health are Non Fiction Books & Adventure
- 777 No One Controls Their Destiny as The Clock Laughs
- 777 Alice in Wonderland, Malice in Blunderland, Chalice in Plunderland
- 777 Soulmate: After The Souls Mate Pay Your Bills
- 777 A whole civilization calls you King or Queen not just your mate
- 777 I Win, Whether we go back to Heaven or descend into Hell, I Win
- 777 Know your Worth

- 777 It's gonna be funny watching peoples attitude adjustments.
- 777 Stay Mysterious Remain Dangerous
- 777 The Memes are lies. A person is whatever they saw their parents do or the reversal thereof.
- 777 Believe the Screen & have No Sol
- 777 We don't have to take over the world together cuss I already Own it. Just Love Me and It's Yours!
- 777 The Problems you face from your mate most likely comes from blood embedded trauma from generations ago therefore they won't change
- 777 Stop thinking like a bum Think like Royalty The World Will be a better place
- 777 Love the Woman Because There's No Other form of Heaven
- 777 To Live in Imagination Is to Stab the Sol
- 777 The Scent that Fumigates from her skin is the Pollen of Creation
- 777 Every Witch just Fulfills the Need
- 777 Respect Animals Because their design is as Immaculate as Yours
- 777 Invisible things like Honor Make up your character more than material things
- 777 To Allow a Woman to be Free Is to Let a Star sit in Outer space
- 777 Spirit is the Religious word Metaphysics is the Scientific word 1 in the same thing
- 777 Her scent is in every part
- 777 There is Never a Mistake It is All called Destiny
- 777 Remain Powerful In Your Way
- 777 I am Human Therefore I Oppose against All
- 777 America is Composed Of 2 Types of People Twittly Dee & Twittly Dumb
- 777 Better start changing your value system
- 777 Move Fast Or The Past Will Last
- 777 Never Believe Enough To be Let Down
- 777 It's a shame the level of intelligence the average human represents
- 777 A Persons surroundings is a Mirror Image of their Mind at Work.
- 777 Ill Taste Her Tears When She Cry & that'll be my Goodbye
- 777 Illusion & Fantasies are so Weak; they can be Slaughtered Overnight Worldwide.
- 777 Pride Is Nothingness
- 777 Luckily I've studied Psychology so well. I can hear Insanity in 1 conversation and will exit left.
- 777 A Disrespectful Mouth Can Never Bring Anything To the Table
- 777 The Fantasies of 1 Mind wont Influence or Change a Million People. Therefore Dreams are Invalid.
- 777 You Must Be ALIVE For the Dead to Speak & See thru You
- 777 Understand the Grandparents of these Indviduals in Gov. Slaughtered your Grandparents & provided your entertainment

- 777 Too Much Information in My Brain Too Much Love in My Heart Too Much Essence in My Sol to be Influenced by some glittery stranger.
- 777 Committ the pointless activity and find the fool in the mirror
- 777 That single momma Syndrome Got you thinking everybody is supposed to care about you.
- 777 Love accepts All, Hate is Limited
- 777 Some people use your sympathy as a high to feed their emptiness from bad decision making.
- 777 Never make assumptions & conclusions without investigating the facts. Otherwise you will loose and look foolish every time.
- 777 I don't like.... Either love or nothing No need for continual games
- 777 The Girl that doesn't Rush Is the Girl that can no longer Blush
- 777 Those who aren't thirsty Get No Water
- 777 Let TV steal your Passions And have No Power to chase, replace, embrace or release a shell case
- 777 Its gonna take a long time for people to see the reality
- 777 Oh yeah: Shrimp sold in America is farmed with pig feces
- 777 Psychology, Sociology & Medical......... The sciences they will never teach you.
- 777 If Dogs & Cats investigate & the human that is designed to do so but does not, he is then what?
- 777 Base your judgments on a screen or reality You Decide
- 777 The Separatists mentality Will be separated
- 777 Never Love a Hag
- 777 Want & Be Wanted Hunt or Be Hunted Say No & Get Nothing
- 777 If Elderly couples don't look at you and your children and smile You're doing it wrong
- 777 Only Respond to Negativity and in essence be negative
- 777 Goddesses are Born, Gods have to Earn the Right
- 777 Let your Animal Acts Reign behind closed doors
- 777 Remember what Love felt like before your scars
- 777 The Horse & The Dog The only 2 animals that will weep for man & are designed for war
- 777 Never disconnect yourself from The Air or The Earth
- 777 Being connected to your woman by Diet & Intellect is as important as sex.
- 777 The Sexual Secretions is the fluid of Psychic Capabilities
- 777 Experience The Plague & Become Emotionally Invincible & Invisible
- 777 If You Can't Survive The Plague, Grunt like Swine in your Grave
- 777 Ladies: You have Coon Coon & Coon Coon is Desired Heal The World
- 777 "Being lit" is a reference to a witch being lit up a stake
- 777 The Ladies Mentalities are changing....... Lawzy Jebus Can a nigga get some oatmeal & some fat back.
- 777 Come to Me, Woman Loose Your Pride & Enjoy Your Sol

- 777 I'm a Witch Doctor An Alchemical Magician You wouldn't Understand
- 777 1 Flutters at your Ear The Other Fly's on a Broom but They Both Conjure at Will
- 777 Her Child like Nature is The Elixir of Art
- 777 There is No Game Only Aim & Attain
- 777 It is ok to be aggressive and softly grab at the throat
- 777 Destroy Your Likes & Your Don't Likes & Become God
- 777 Power is defined by the thigh master
- 777 Sink Your Teeth In Since You are Thirsty Quench your Sol & Breathe Again
- 777 I love being thirsty and hunting. I get what's made for me or I'll make it for me.
- 777 You will Bend as Metal against a Torch and shall be Pounded into Fine Weaponry
- 777 Don't hurt the sol Or play with the heart Jump in her mind and play your part
- 777 Keep child's play a mile away
- 777 Those who aren't serious Can only be delirious
- 777 Never eaten Ramen noodles or chitlins
- 777 I never really did music for money or fame. I do it cuss Hip Hop & Legends Died & I stayed at their Grave. Alone
- 777 Always Remember A Screen Name is a No – Body Literally
- 777 B Tactical & Speedy Analytical & Greedy Miracles Yes Indeedy Cynical & Impeding
- 777 I Loved You When You Didn't Know what Love Was I Killed You to put You Out of your Misery And that's Love
- 777 Look back at your life Understand There was never "the one" just "the one" for that time period.
- 777 I don't do that lean on me shit.......... Don't think you can lean on me...........
- 777 It is better to attain the material possession. Than the mind changing human.
- 777 Let your Pride, Hide & Confide, In the Ride
- 777 The Earth only Keeps who She Needs or Loves from reciprocation. The rest will be discarded. It's called Natural Selection
- 777 It's ok to be far ahead. You'll only unify with others who are. The connection will be far greater and longer.
- 777 All Hearts Beat in Darkness As No Light Enters the Human body.
- 777 The Eyes are The Steering Wheel Of the Mind
- 777 She Fears the One who can make her Fall in Love. Only because She Thinks she won't be able to make him do anything.
- 777 To be Dead and Rise again Is an Ancient Metaphor For Erectile dysfunction

- 777 Having to live in so many places during life. You learn how to stay detached, no human is reliable. Make your situation guaranteed
- 777 Think about the results before the action Unless a skull needs cracking
- 777 In the Medieval Times.... Executioners would say they beheaded the criminal as a "favor". To release one from their misery. Understand the language. To work for somebody else is a status of slavery. To be laid off is a "favor" to let you be free of responsibility.
- 777 Being Experienced Kills Excitement
- 777 Never attempt to change a person
- 777 Never taunt or tease Because true hunger is never at ease
- 777 Everything in existence is a concept you can either add it to you or subtract it from you
- 777 Make sure you Lick Her Sol, Finger Her Mind and Massage Her Heart when you talk to her.
- 777 Beg Each other Its so much more ENTICING
- 777 I don't wear a mask, I know how the earth & existence works, which trumps a plague
- 777 You can only defeat a thing like money or the plague when you fall in love with it or make love to it.
- 777 Once she gives you her jugular vein for your teeth's sinking. She is yours.
- 777 If her eyes aint wide and bright like a runaway slave sticking her head out the bushes. You aint hit the coon coon right.
- 777 Oh baby...... You, You got what I neeeed, & You say its Quarantine, You say its Quarantined
- 777 I don't get disturbed by the cops, they nod their head and shake my hand whether quarantine or not
- 777 It is Time To Descend 72 Angels & Devils
- 777 You are Here To Conquer All Dimensions Of The Psyche
- 777 Self-Discipline Is The Sharpness of The Blade & The Tip of The Bullet
- 777 Money Is the GREATEST WEAPON
- 777 Weak Minds & Weak Hearts are both 1 in the same.
- 777 A True Man of Purpose cannot choose Love over Losing.
- 777 Socialism is The Analog Matrix
- 777 Beauty is A Magic System
- 777 Work Things Out Figure Things Out & Survive
- 777 Achieve Immortality In Your Revenge
- 777 Common ground is the marble floor only the wise walk upon
- 777 Eagles only See Eye to Eye With Other Eagles
- 777 If your situation Is complication Create a new destination
- 777 You are supposed to Hear Each other's Heart During Sex
- 777 Try to stop the planets alignments And they will align Against you
- 777 I love it when butchs look at me and understand they are nowhere near a man Know your place

- 777 Care about those who care about themselves and be progressive
- 777 If you don't want to mix genetically Don't mix at all
- 777 Enough of her squirting will become a layer to your aura
- 777 Dominate the woman behind all women And Understand The Human Sol
- 777 Only The Bold Girl Travels The Woods Alone
- 777 Her scent & her colors Are her Mating call
- 777 Tell Me. Has that Hamsters wheel in your mind created light yet?
- 777 Americanism The first culture in human existence to not have forced maturity development rituals
- 777 Rely on Destiny
- 777 Enforcing your Intelligence on Fools Is telling the blind to look
- 777 Fear is the lack of confidence in one's self defense Whether that be mental or physical
- 777 All The Ladies Are Born with Great Raunch seeking The Debauch
- 777 A Woman's Orgasm Is really a Television Screen of Her Imagination & Dreams
- 777 Hesitation is a Result of the Inadequacy of Investigation & Calculation
- 777 Read My Mind As I Walk Your Sol Woman And Let No Heart be Chained
- 777 There is Always a Reason
- 777 Entrepreneur Men Have no time for foul mouthed women. It's a waste of energy. Energy is valuable.
- 777 The woman that only dreams of a baby and family still has an outdated tribal mind.
- 777 Your words are magic. Frequency penetrates. Shit talking creates shit Attacks at your character restricts progress.
- 777 I don't deal with What Ifs & Maybes Make the Shit Happen Or Get The Fuck Out The Way
- 777 I don't understand no grown ass mafucca talking bout they aint responsible
- 777 Funny how single mothers expect single fathers to be as sloppy as they are....
- 777 The Top Euphoria Humans are designed to experience is Love. This can be crippled by wrong birth practices or upbringing trauma
- 777 Reasons others may be jealous: you were raised with both parents, far more travled or experienced or even if you were breast fed
- 777 The herb fennel is what was used to be thrown at weddings not rice. Fennel also assists in breast milk.
- 777 The ancient and correct way of child delivery is squatting not laying on your back.
- 777 Everything is Mathematical
- 777 Hear Ones Voice And Know Their Sol, See Ones Text & Confuse Yourself
- 777 Money doesn't remove the energy you create from being an asshole

- 777 I don't know how to deal with insane people nor will I try to figure it out jus cuss 'em out and discard. Fan or Not.
- 777 St. Homobonus is The Patron Saint of Pimping, St. Vitalis of Gaza is The Patron Saint of Prostitutes & Johns Welcome to Las Vegas
- 777 We Live in a world designed by a collective illusion from a hi off of sugar, coffee, liquor, tobacco/weed, cocaine & booty.
- 777 Study, Debate & Become
- 777 The Root Word for God is the German Word Guut. Your Guts nervous system is designed just like your brain. Above as Below.
- 777 The First Pendulum were the mothers swinging breasts
- 777 The Aquarian is unnecessary with their defiance that they project as revolution and seeks comfort more than gain
- 777 Capricorn means Horn of The Goat & The Constellation is shaped like the Horn of a Goat. It is also the most sexually immoral mammal. By our standards, hence animals have no concept of morals.
- 777 Pisces usually have slim heads like fish are slim & also aren't keen on control or relationships because fish are rarely monogamous.
- 777 Both The Libra & Scorpio have shapes that take after The Uterus of The Virgo who is the sweetness of the Lions Roar & the consequence of Law
- 777 Taurus Moon = Made of Cheese = Gold in The Year of The Rat
- 777 Thirst Trap = Mental Spider Web = Headache = Witchcraft = Worthlessness
- 777 There is No such thing as Whoredom, You're either making love or making hate, PLAY BALL!
- 777 The Woman That Applies Force to Be in Your Life, Does Not Seek Money
- 777 Sheeeesh, I can't drive to the store Without somebody Yellin at me
- 777 God Bless The Rebel That Wears No Mask
- 777 Taweret The Egyptian Goddess Wants to "Be With You", Women Only
- 777 The Greek Goddess Hygeia who lives inside the word Hygeine wanted to say Hello, in The Time of Plague
- 777 Lunatic is Lunar which is also Lupus. Lupus a skin/joint disease connected to Werewolfism in ancient times.
- 777 Our Sun is a Double mirror image of a sun 1500 times larger call VY Canis Majoris also where we get the words canine and cannabis
- 777 The word Equinox comes from Equine which is the Horse. Same with Nightmare Mare is Horse
- 777 There are 88 zodiac signs in our extended solar system.
- 777 Virgo is the secret keeper. As is the Mother, as is her Womb. Her witch side is called a Virago.
- 777 Libras will always be good at music. As music is 1 of the frequency laws of human existence.
- 777 Scorpios are natural eavesdroppers and snoopers. Remember insects are the fly's on the wall in the room.

- 777   Winter signs are cold in Nature as Nature is Cold during Winter. Scorpio, Sagittarius & Capricorn.
- 777   January is Named After the Greek God Janus who is Capricious (a 2 sided thinker) like Capricorn.
- 777   Geminis can find justification in both sides of an argument. But always leans on Justice. The Roman God Mercury rules Gemini & Thieves.
- 777   The Taurus represents Gold Cows & Women were the first form of Money amongst Man. The Bull & The Man takes their time with both.
- 777   Aires like Leo the Beginning & End of The Sun should work in jobs related with human communication. Everybody needs their Royal Essence.
- 777   Cancers make sure others are well fed. Especially while working, they have aggressive minds. The majority of the mob were Cancers.
- 777   Taurus represents The morning Sun from 9 - 12 am. They support the phrase "Early Bird Gets The Worm".
- 777   Every Woman controls a Dimension
- 777   The Masculine season is from Aires – Leo, The Feminine season is from Virgo – Pisces.
- 777   The Attempt to Figure Out someone else's thinking or reasoning doesn't pay.
- 777   The Human Mind Will Always Change About Everything
- 777   Will Power is All 1 Has.
- 777   Be Infatuated
- 777   Philosophy, Fighting, Chasing, Catching & Dominating Is How Boys Become Men
- 777   Internet unions will never be as strong as love at first site.
- 777   There's a thin line between Tough & Stupid
- 777   The truth is, your money is your talent. And 9 × outta 10, Your mate isn't going to have similar or related talents.
- 777   I'm Not Wearing No God Damn Mask...... You Get Your God Damn Hands Off of Me
- 777   When The Fire is Out There's No More Warmth
- 777   All Healers are prepared for Scars
- 777   It was called The Dancing Mania.... It only occured in Old Europe during The Medieval times. It went on for 350 - 400 years. Insane Dancing until the breaking of bones or death from exhaustion. The spirit of the crackhead dancing on the corner and maybe even twerking was developed in this practice.
- 777   If you aint tryna get rid of your problems Keep 'em to yourself
- 777   You need more than beauty
- 777   Little Red Riding Hood Will Only Tip Toe Towards a Wolf
- 777   Silence brings more prosperity than a bad bitch with a foul mouth
- 777   When you have no Judgment skills. You just remain a coward to everything and skeptically create excuses to not involve yourself
- 777   People who don't have a Value system, have no Desire or Hunt

- 777 A tight family unit & a bunch of socially inadequate dumbasses living off of eachother are not the same thing.
- 777 Lemme find out you've been living the big willy lifestyle online but never left mommas house.
- 777 Humans pay Bills, Animals don't.
- 777 Sanity is Proven by the capacity to maintain bills not surviving. Hence beggars who are usually insane still survive.
- 777 When you classify someone as insane. Everything they do is justified because they are insane.
- 777 The Man that wants to Control his woman Is No Boss.
- 777 Be Quick to Identify those who don't have a Value system which means they don't have a decision making prowess. Stay Away!
- 777 The real reason for this stimulus is the next generations are to stupid to maintain the country
- 777 The Battlefield of Art Is The Tug of War Over The Humans Sol. Who has the Intelligence of an Animal.
- 777 Men have to Take Sols, Women have to Give Sols
- 777 During The Plague, I gotta AK & a Slave
- 777 If Her Love isn't similar to a Girl checking the mailman everyday for a letter from her man off at war. Its a waste of time.
- 777 Break the format of 10,000yrs of human communication and cause mental health issues on 7 billion people.
- 777 For those who wanna run around, remember when the dog chases his tail he also Runs around..........
- 777 A Lady loves a man enforcing her femininity with order A raunch will try to despise it & run away
- 777 Always check a person's value & accomplishment rate before considering their games
- 777 My definition of knowing somebody is based on thriving with them, Your definition is seeing their social media We are not the same
- 777 The fool: How you gone tell me about God, I had an experience, he talked to me, Me: that was actually a tapeworm
- 777 There is more communication done with the eyes, clothing and posture than there is with words.
- 777 Modern sciences say there are 21 Facial Expressions, Ancient sciences say there are 264 You Decide?!?!?!?!?
- 777 Every Politician Competes with Jesus For their Space in History
- 777 Provide Ones Blanket & Pillow Then Dance in Their Dreams
- 777 There is No Social Order There is Only Your Time & The Times
- 777 Nyctimene (Night time) is a Roman Goddess represented as an Owl Her name has been given to a genus of bats
- 777 Samoan Mythology Is the Only System With a Bat Goddess Her name is Leutogi

- 777 Synthetic, Computer Generated Sounds destroy the thinking patterns of brains that are built only for natural sounds
- 777 If you want a Clear Mind only drink water, authentic fruit juices and herbal teas
- 777 Be Blind to those You give pain and Be The Vampire who has no Reflection in the Mirror.
- 777 Those who take hold to fantasy in their youth will grow old to find insanity in their hand.
- 777 As an Adult it is Wise to be attracted to ones accomplishments as much as the person. Because possessions can come from anywhere.
- 777 Convincing someone Is a waste of time Its either they Desire & have Will Power or Don't
- 777 When you Understand that her Orgasm is 1,000 yrs of what's in her family line, inclusive with thoughts & food. The Game Changes.
- 777 Always Remember History Proves Those who want & start revolutions. Don't have the intelligence to rebirth society. PLAY BALL
- 777 Alota Spiders with Nothing in their Webs Tsk, Tsk, Tsk
- 777 About the recent Police Shootings.........You'll continue to be treated like animals until you PROVIDE FOR YOUR OWN & to OTHER RACES both Industrially and Agriculturally like HUMANS DO.
- 777 They've degenerated people's minds by media and their bodies by food to a point to deteriorate yourself by your own thoughts
- 777 I feel the Wind from your Wings Grace
- 777 Desire has to be high rate on both parties hands for a successful long relationship.
- 777 The woman you chase is in essence, running. Once caught she will run again.
- 777 For the agreeable & progressive, words are the only force you need
- 777 Dieu ne se donne qu'a l'amour
- 777 Exercise, Astrology, News, Stocks, Read Before the kids wake up, Everyday
- 777 Stingy Bourgeois, Cynical Peasants & Loveless Intellectuals
- 777 If you encounter multiple women of the same name understand it is the spirit/goddess/principle that comes for you, not the woman.
- 777 Blame things that go wrong in your relationship on astrology, time & change & ya'll will be fine.
- 777 Consistency & Respect is before Likes & Emotions PLAY BALL
- 777 Angra Mainyu Is The Demon that lives In the word Angry
- 777 Opus Proprium
- 777 Nobody is Ever their True Self, Everybody Will Change
- 777 The Human is a Flesh Computer operated by liquids & memory
- 777 What's in a person's name is who they are Welcome to the Matrix

- 777 When You Have to Breathe for The Dead & Fight The Invisible for The Living
- 777 Life Turned Upside Down Planet Topsy Turvy
- 777 Terminator Don't Need No Ventilator
- 777 Either Play the Game of Thrones Or live in a broken happy home
- 777 It is better to inspect before you expect
- 777 It is better to not desire then to be disappointed
- 777 Never impose that you are wanted and discover otherwise
- 777 If you're thinking produces no fruit it is inadequate
- 777 Value & Worth The Only Judgment Call
- 777 Past repetition predicts The Future
- 777 Money doesn't remove the energy you create from being an asshole
- 777 I'm a fulfill your dreams woman, Because you already put me there
- 777 Always remember Ladies: You want to Render Men as Useless for a Dollar Bill that has a Man's face on it. PLAY BALL
- 777 When You Feed You Bleed, When You Read You Succeed PLAY BALL
- 777 The woman that thinks her children are in debt to her screams. Will end up the lonely fool.
- 777 The Woman that responds to Her Age accordingly, by her actions, attitude, force & submission. WILL HAVE NO WORRY
- 777 The Ones that make sure they Win. Are also the ones that had no pride to do so. They understood their position.
- 777 Relationship: the attempt to control the person that made you feel like you're on top of the world until said feeling burns out
- 777 So What Make Moves
- 777 For those who want and don't achieve Want nothing indeed
- 777 The Soldier focuses on Winning the Battle The King focuses on Winning the War
- 777 Common Ground is The Basis of Marriage, Divorce & The Boardroom PLAY BALL
- 777 Arguments & Violence Does not Define Love But it does Define your intelligence
- 777 Sex is best left at 2 times a month for a healthy long money focused relationship
- 777 The Quality of Work you Do Is also The Quantity of Dollars you Make
- 777 Remember Men: They ALL Report to the Command Center/Battle Station, The Great Sabbat to Receive Instructions from The Goat
- 777 When you get what you want in front of people who want but don't get They run off
- 777 While you think you are testing someone with a game, the game is testing you.
- 777 Claim The Throne Or Complain & Moan

- 777 When you Destroy your Position of Being Wanted, You Will also Remove yourself from Being Needed
- 777 Build the Desire & Cherish The First Bite
- 777 Learn Ones Past & The Skeletons in the closet dance.
- 777 The Law don't Make Love
- 777 It is usually the inexperienced or the ultra-experienced that have long lasting relationships
- 777 Only the Weak Cant stay Consistent On their Desires
- 777 Dementia & Hysteria In female older age Is very real
- 777 Lay Out your Cards when you're interested in someone, even your ills. To Discover Great Stench later is so disheartening.
- 777 Accept Your Mates Devils before their Angels and your relationship will succeed
- 777 When You Figure Out, What You Thought Was a Dream, Is An Ordered Mission......
- 777 They know you are Soulless. So they provide a realm where you can be the soul to a character in a false world. Whallah... Now you're a somebody in a world of nothingness.
- 777 To know a woman's soul by looking in her eyes and can call her souls name and she respond with a smile is an astounding feeling
- 777 The Creative Principles: Will, Wisdom & Activity
- 777 So the Fear of Love creates High Anxiety in women. So if the Media tells women they have Anxiety and they enforce it to play out, by default they also incorporate the fear of love. Which is also the lack of communication and attention span.
- 777 I can only believe What I know
- 777 Revolutions   Occur every 3 years since the 1700's. It's a social software program of nothingness
- 777 Only People who have no business destroy other people's business
- 777 Stereotype = Software for Humans
- 777 Yes, you are living in Thee Matrix... Anybody wearing a mask or connected to any new social hype a Mr. Smith can show up thru.
- 777 The Ladies ensure a male's weakness and emasculate them so they can be heard.........
- 777 You can't Be Progressive Without Being Aggressive
- 777 Fuck all that new booty hate, separation, support the degenerate, laughing and jeering shit you operate by. Ill never do it.
- 777 The Strongest form of support to a Man is a Woman's Excitement & Happiness
- 777 If you don't conduct enough human activity you will not be treated as one This is Law
- 777 There is No Fortune Without Taking The Penance

777   A woman does keep you on edge about your work...... In her absence coffee is the substitute.

777   Work fuck work fuck work fuck work fuck work fuck work fuck work fuck So goes a mans life

777   Be Agreeable & Pleasant & Win Your Defiance is The Stench of a Loser Esta La Rotten Carcass

777   All Propositions are Real

777   To Bad You Allowed Your Mind to be filled with Bullshit over 20 yrs & you cant make proper decisions.

777   You cannot Sail the Ocean of Love in a Ship..... One can Only Swim in The Boundless Waters

777   Let The Cheeks Of every Mary Blush In Innocence & Passion

777   Let God Bless The Green Rosary Beads St. Benedict of Nursia, St. Benedict The Moor, St. Catherine of Siena & St. Corona

777   To Need Another is both Natural & Painful

777   There is Only Thought. Hence: Once upon a Time Someone or Something, Somewhere Thought of the Human Design

777   In this Dimension only animals are born with physical weapons for offense & defense. The Human only has their Mind.

777   Remember after an Animal eats it can only watch........

777   It is better to externalize the council in your mind to entities you create or you embody them in your friends

777   Small Efforts are Never seen by Giants or Large Audiences

777   Power is an Invisible Thing that must be Identified, Hunted & Attained

777   In a relationship the woman tries to get the man to think like the woman and the man make the woman think like a man

777   Philosophy Is The Love of Sophistication

777   The Black Male The Most Duplicated And The Most Hated Amongst the Entire Human Race

777

777   Happiness is a Wanted Goal it is not a requirement of survival or to exist.

777   Is it societal influence or is it lack of education and experience that makes women fear men or both?

777   The Human is Only a Filter whatever goes in must come out in all forms

777   Provide & Be Ignored

777   The Lady is a Pretty Bird A Real Man is an Oak Tree

777   Emotional Attachment? The Great Illusion

777   Her Squirt Juice WILL turn you into the type of men in her family, if they're bums you will turn into a bum via her DNA.

777   Everybody on my line trying to get me to think this way or that way

777   I Lost Desire & Want For You But Thats The Way You Wanted It

777   When the world wants You 2 to be together What do you do?

777   P.M.S Persuade Manipulate Seduce

- 777 Procure & Pursue
- 777 On the Battlefield of Entertainment Principles, Sounds, Shapes, Time, Colors & Numbers are Our Weapons
- 777 Once upon a time in America the term "thick" was used to refer to stupidity. Hence: "Thick in the head"
- 777 A rich sol has no worry As an empty body worries everyone
- 777 A Mans Mind and Heart must be fulfilled as much as a woman's playful spirit and under garments
- 777 You Must Conquer Complication in Order to Simplify
- 777 Woman: The Only Meat That Prepares Its Self for Its Own Slaughter - Medieval Math
- 777 See Your Dreams Fall in Love with Reality Only then Can You Design Your Future
- 777 Only those Who Understand Existence Can actually Exist
- 777 What If I told you: You're Sol is actually a Criminal from another constellation, your body a jail & your Emotions your punishment
- 777 Does an animal understand their existence in nature greater than a human understands their existence in a city
- 777 A Lie is Only a Deep Cut To The Flesh As A Failed Illusion Is a Stab to an Organ
- 777 Babies that aren't breastfed have problems with affection and love later in life.
- 777 A Product Must Be Designed to Be Alive and Walk on its Own
- 777 If You Do Not Understand Magic Don't Waste Your Time with Business
- 777 Never Expect Sympathy as a Response in Business
- 777 To Be Blind is The Progression of Man
- 777 Swim in The Ocean with No Care of What Lurks below
- 777 If there is No Path in The Woods, Then Watch Your Step
- 777 To Pimp with Compassion is to Love the Mother Goddess of All Women
- 777 Grace is the only way to Ice Skate in Politics
- 777 Success is an Oasis of Stress
- 777 If you and your mates upbringing aren't of the same financial class, it won't work and you're concealing traumas from the past
- 777 Because there is astrology & balance. Some people are born darksided and all of your ills are predestined.
- 777 I'm solution & progressive oriented. If you're gonna wish & dream all day talking about your desires and not get 'em go rot somewhere
- 777 A Lady asked for help on how she educate her daughters about sex as one of them was already active.

    I responded: You teach her about her vagina inside and out. You teach her about the sexual psychological dynamics of males. You teach her about courting from victorian age until now here in America. You teach her about Etiquette. You teach her about oils and herbs that keep her healthy. You teach both of them. If you dont know, then you sit down and all of you learn together. Teach them emotional control and human behaviors that symbolize traumas that may be in her mate. Oh yeah a couple things about pregnancy would be good review this information over time.

- 777 The Woman that makes herself stay with a Monster is the True Revolutionary
- 777 Tease a Lion And become the Meal
- 777 Integrity is Everything Money is Temporary Reputation is Memory
- 777 When you ask for Angels, remember they had to Fall in Order to get to you.
- 777 The truth to the matter is: Women don't know what a man is, so they scared as fuck of falling in love and having to fulfill duties.
- 777 Love is to be felt and not owned
- 777 Ladiness is written in her words & acts, motherliness & good pussy is written in her face & thighs, health is in her shape & scent
- 777 Always Remember Everything is Politics
- 777 Incels.... They're a bunch of lames who feel as if they should blow up the world because they don't get any sex or even attention from women. This is an age old problem with human existence. In yesteryear women were traded for cows and these problems didn't persist. Civilization was built and maintained. Just like the rules of engagement between the sexes during the founding of America, women were once desirable and orderly, but the men kept them that way with many different tactics. Unfortunately, women are now running rabid, men are emasculated and all of civilization is collapsing. Ladies..... Always remember the Love you possess and the energy you give, is more important than you specifically. Men need it and if neglected from it or it is unachievable other drastic measures will be taken.
- 777 Sympathy for The single mother is the drive of mankind
- 777 Being Selfish Will Bring You Closer to being Homeless Then Selflessness
- 777 Humiliate Yourself & Be Prideless, In Your Progression
- 777 A Rose, She'd rather Not Feel The Thorns that are Unknown to her.
- 777 Accept Your Mates Bad, As Much as Their Good And Love Forever
- 777 Force is The Communication of Lovers
- 777 Those who are Stubborn Receive The Rug Burn
- 777 The Mind is The Brain of The Spirit, The Brain is The Controller of The Flesh
- 777 The Consequences of Evil Acts Come from The Atmosphere
- 777 As Everything you Purchase Has Instructions or an Instruction Manual. Life has a Library
- 777 Im in your heart whether you like it or not were connected whether you like it or not
- 777 Either Cooperate Or Coagulate
- 777 To Not Breathe and Be Alive is The Superiority of Technology.

- 777 The Clock is The Heart Beat of The Robot.
- 777 There is No such thing as Time. There is only Monkey See, Monkey Do.
- 777 Its better to Operate off of Knowing Instead of Optimisim & Guessing
- 777 Love is the answer that nobody wants
- 777 Trust me: There are more unspoken/invisible rules to making a million then there are both spoken & written combined.
- 777 Remember Usually Only Men travel up and down the financial/social levels. Women just represent the levels that they stay on.
- 777 I didn't scare you to turn you off, I scared you so nobody else would be able to, Now Be Bold & Daring
- 777 Women can only get you mad when your inexperienced with them, emotionally driven, depend on them & your money low.
- 777 The Negro: Tears down statues of old racist soldiers. Failing to realize his great grandchildren run shit now
- 777 Ladies: You ain't important enough to kill. Stop thinking every man wanna hurt you.
- 777 The True Woman Smiles at Perversion! Why you may ask? What Stallion doesn't blitzkrieg a Battlefield?
- 777 Only those who are to weak to enforce Order have a problem with Order being enforced.
- 777 When you have no self-control, you cannot control anything outside yourself.
- 777 Understand, only unsuccessful criminals, who get caught, have a problem with the police.
- 777 If A Butch doesn't Look at you like you're a Cop and she's the criminal on the run with the warrant, You're NOT a Man.
- 777 To Act during The Animal Act Is to Rush The Blood
- 777 If a woman dont adjust her shit, check her kids and straighten her clothes when she sees you. Youre not a Man.
- 777 MEN: You can only be angry if you are in jail, majorly injured or your money has been effected. Anything else is Feminine.
- 777 Time for Her is Forever Ever After
- 777 So If The Sun cant Pierce Inside The Internet, same as The Human Body, It is exclusively a Dark World
- 777 Inside The Word Riot Lives The God Rudra He has Now been Disembowled
- 777 You only know somebody after you fight em or fuck em.
- 777 Fear and Confusion is Attached to The Psychological Structure Of a Womans Orgasm
- 777 Pride & Ignored Requests are The Author to Loneliness
- 777 A Man's Anger at a Woman or Women is a Defense mechanism to guard himself from falling in love and loosing himself

- ☤ To Allow Yourself to Be Conquered by Another is in itself Accepting the Strength of Another it is not conquering or defeat
- ☤ The Woman's True Teachings are Done with Her Silence
- ☤ When you walk up the mountain, you will be able to appreciate the view longer.
- ☤ The People are Bright, The People are Buzzing, The People are Beautiful
- ☤ If you can't compromise or come to a common ground, youre not relationship material
- ☤ The Mind is The Brain of The Spirit, The Brain is Controls The Flesh
- ☤ The Consequences of Evil Acts, Come from The Atmosphere
- ☤ As Everything you Purchase Has Instructions or an Instruction Manual, Life has a Library
- ☤ Realization: There is Nothing that is Fake because It is in Existence & Everything that Exists is Real
- ☤ To be real white people operate off of complex sciences that others dont understand. Fortunately the majority of it is right.
- ☤ Only operate in the public with those that you communicate with in private.
- ☤ There is No such thing as Time. There is only Monkey See, Monkey Do.
- ☤ You are really looking at the battle between 50 yrs of technology influenced communication against 10,000 years of human behavior
- ☤ Men: A Woman's Psyche/Mind has No Comprehension of Winning. There are no experiences in their gender history thats competitive.
- ☤ Pussy is Thee Maintenance of Male Sanity
- ☤ So let me get this right: The rioters are wearing masks while rioting against the establishment that told them to wear masks.
- ☤ Relationships only last long when the woman has no pride to chase the man only because the woman gets chased by every man
- ☤ Animals Have no Recognition of their Organs as a Humans care for their Hair is more important then their brain.
- ☤ You are witnessing, Motherly Love, And Fatherly Lack, The Virgin Mary can't Stop The Violence of Man. The Mother Mary will only Cry. The Black Madonna turns a Blind Eye.
- ☤ It is the Demon who is Happy with Fire reflecting in the Eyes as the smile stretches from pointed ear to pointed ear
- ☤ Reading provides silence & secrecy, Silence & secrecy Provides mystery of Attack
- ☤ Play with this line and the Results are Ugly
- ☤ Role Playing Is The Private Jet of The Mind
- ☤ You can't run like a coward and expect to be treated as an equal
- ☤ You must pass the realm of birthing and controlling a family before attempting to run a corporation.
- ☤ To Not Breathe and Be Alive is The Superiority of Technology.

Chapter 7: The Word

Se7en: Gk *hepta.* An English prefix, as in *heptachord, heptad, heptagon, hebdomad, hebdomadary.* (Donne, in a 1631 sermon,. Spoke scornfully of the hebdomadary righteous: those that deem good behavior on Sunday sufficient for the week.) L *septem. Septan, septangular, septennial septuple.* Septemberist was one of the revolutionists that massacred royalists in Paris in Spet. 1792. The term was also applied to the Portuguese, who in Sept. 1836 brought about the restoration of the country's 1822 constitution. Black September is the group of Arab terrorists (an outgrowth of al-Fatah, heard by Abd al-Rahman abd al-rauf Arafat al-Qud al Husseinie before he took command of the PLO, Palestine Liberation Organization) which has sought to avenge the unexpected defeat of Syrian and guerrilla forces in what it calls "Black September," 1970; the group pledged to attack not olf in Israel but all over the world, its most spectacular strike to date being the killing of 11 Israeli atheletes at the 1972 Olympic Games in Munich.

OED lists 45 and details 18 relevant words beginning hept(a), Heptamerous; Hebdo, as *hebdomically*: according to the mystical number seven. It lists 7 and details 37 relevant words beginning sept, as septemfluous; flowing in seven branches, as does the Nile; septenary.

Gc, seven, seventh, seventeen, seventy, etc.

> Seven cities* warr'd for Homer, being dead,
> Who living, had no roof to shroud his head.
> -Thomas Heywood, Hierarchie of the
> Blessed angels (1635)

Note that septum comes from L sepire, septum: to divide; a hedge, also amembrane. And septic(a)emia comes from Gk *septikhos: putrefying (plus haima: blood); whence also septic, septicine, , septicity, aseptic, antiseptic.*

Septentrion(es) is a name for the seven brightest stars (visible to the naked eye) of the constellation Ursa Major, the Great Bear, a circumpolar group in the northern sky which never sets. To the Hindus, these stars represent the seven Rashis, the great sages. In Greek legend Callisto was a nymph serving Artemis; she bore Zeusa son, Arcus (ancestor of the Arcadians), and angry Artemis changed her into a bear. When Arcus was about to slay the bear, Zeus changed Callisto into the into the Great Bear constellation, and set her son Arcus into the near sky as Arcturus: guardian of the bear (in the constellation Arctophylas, with the same meaning). The Star Arcturus speaks the prologue in Plautus's play Rudens [The Rope], 194 B.C., perhaps the masterpiece of Roman comedy.

Other names are used for Septentrion. It may be called the Wagon; when Arcturus is called Bootes: the Wagoner. The early word for wagon was wain, and the constellation was alson called churl's (peasent's) wain. This was later folk changed to Charles's Wain (by association with King Charlemagne) because of its nearness to Arcturus, which was similarly folk-understood as Arcturus, for King Arthur, who is linked in legend with Charlemagne. Homer, in the Odyssey, v, mentions "the Great Bear, by others called the Wain," In Shakespeare's 1 Henry IV, II, 1, the hour of night is judged by the fact that "Charles' Wain is over the new chimney." The group of seven is more commonly known today as the Big Dipper.

"The sluggard is wiser in his own conceit than seven men that can render a reason"-Bible, Proverbs 26:16.

> As I was going to St. Ives
> I met a man with seven wives,
> Each wife had seven sacks,
> Each sack had seven cars,
> Each cat had seven kits;
> Kits, cats, sacks, and wives,
> How many were going to St. Ives?
> -Nursery riddle, 1720 [70]

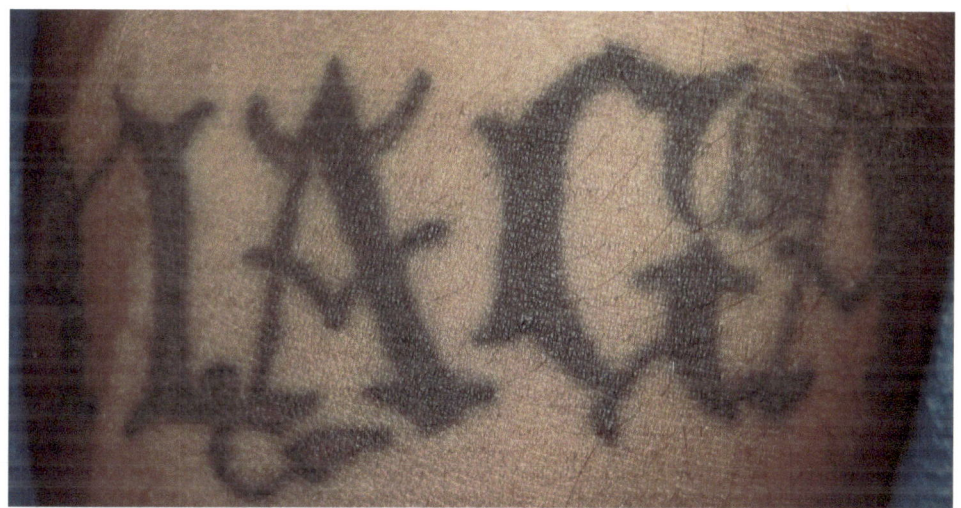

7:) Naga Tattoo located on the Inner Left Arm of Keenan Booker

Se7en: The ordinary Sanskrit words for the number seven are *sapta* and *saptan*. Here is a list of corresponding numerical symbols: *Abdhi, Achala, *Adri, *Aga, *Ashva, *Atri, Bhaya, Bhubhrit, *Bhudhara, Chandas, Dhatu, Dhi, *Dvipa, *Giri, Haya, Kalatra, *Loka, *Mahidhara, *Matrika, *Muni, *Naga, *Parvata, *Patala, *Pavana, *Pushkara, *Rishi, *sagara, *Sagaram *Samudra, *Shaila, *Svara, *Tattva, *Turaga, *Turangama, *Vajin, *Vara, *Vyasana* and *Yati*. These words have the following symbolic meaning or translation:

7. "Purification" and by extension "Purifier" (*Pavana*). 2. The Horses (*Ashva, Turaga, Turangama, Vajin*). 3. The island continents (*Dvipa*). 4. The seas or oceans (*Sagara, Samurdra*). 5. The divine Mothers (*Matrika*). 6. The Worlds (*Loka*). 7. The Inferior Worlds (*Patala*). 8. The Mountains or Hills (*Adri, Aga, Bhubhrit, Bhudhara, Giri, Mahidhara, Naga, Paravata, Shaila*). 9. The

syllables (*Svara*). 10. The musical notes (*Svara*). 11. The "Sages" of Vedic times (*Muni, Rishi*). 12. The last of the seven Rishi (*Atri*). 13. The days of the week (Vara). 14. "That which does not move" (*Naga*). 15. The 7th "island continent" (*Pushkara*). The fears (*Bhaya*) 17. The winds (*Pavana*). [71]

A deep significance was attached to numbers in hoary antiquity. There was not a people with anything like philosophy, but gave great prominence to numbers in their application to religious observances, the establishment of festival days, symbols, dogmas, and even the geographical distribution of empires. The mysterious numerical system of Pythagoras was nothing novel when it appeared far earlier than 600 years B.C. The occult meaning of figures and their combinations entered into the meditations of the sages of every people; and the day is not far off when, compelled by the eternal cyclic rotation of events, our now sceptical unbelieving West will have to admit that in that regular periodicity of ever recurring events there is something more than a mere blind chance. Already our Western savants begin to notice it. Of late, they have pricked up their ears and begun speculating upon cycles, numbers and all that which, but a few years ago, they had relegated to oblivion in the old closets of memory, never to be unlocked but for the purpose of grinning at the uncouth and idiotic superstitions of our unscientific forefathers.

As one of such novelties, the old, and matter-of-fact German journal Die Gegenwart has a serious and learned article upon "the significance of the number seven" introduced to the readers as a "Culture-historical Essay." After quoting from it a few extracts, we will have something to add to it perhaps. The author says:

The number seven was considered sacred not only by all the cultured nations of antiquity and the East, but was held in the greatest reverence even by the later nations of the West. The astronomical origin of this number is established beyond any doubt. Man, feeling himself time out of mind dependent upon the heavenly powers, ever and everywhere made earth subject to heaven. The largest and brightest of the luminaries thus became in his sight the most important and highest of powers; such were the planets which the whole antiquity numbered as seven. In course of time these were transformed into seven deities. The Egyptians had seven original and higher gods; the Phœnicians seven kabiris; the Persians, seven sacred horses of Mithra; the Parsees, seven angels opposed by seven demons, and seven celestial abodes paralleled by seven lower regions. To represent the more clearly this idea in its concrete form, the seven gods were often represented as one seven-headed deity. The whole heaven was subjected to the seven planets; hence, in nearly all the religious systems we find seven heavens.

The beliefs in the sapta loka of the Brahminical religion has remained faithful to the archaic philosophy; and--who knows--but the idea itself was originated in Aryavarta, this cradle of all philosophies and mother of all subsequent religions! If the Egyptian dogma of the metempsychosis or the transmigration of soul taught that there were seven states of purification and progressive perfection, it is also true that the Buddhists took from the Aryans of India, not from Egypt, their idea of seven stages of progressive development of the disembodied soul, allegorized by the seven stories and umbrellas, gradually diminishing towards the top on their pagodas.

In the mysterious worship of Mithra there were "seven gates," seven altars, seven mysteries. The priests of many Oriental nations were sub-divided into seven degrees; seven steps led to the altars and in the temples burnt candles in seven-branched candlesticks. Several of the Masonic Lodges have, to this day, seven and fourteen steps.

The seven planetary spheres served as a model for state divisions and organizations. China was divided into seven provinces; ancient Persia into seven satrapies. According to the Arabian legend seven angels cool the sun with ice and snow, lest it should burn the earth to cinders; and seven thousand angels wind up and set the sun in motion every morning. The two oldest rivers of the East--the Ganges and the Nile--had each seven mouths. The East had in the antiquity seven principal rivers (the Nile, the Tigris, the Euphrates, the Oxus, the Yaksart, the Arax and the Indus); seven famous treasures; seven cities full of gold; seven marvels of the world, &c. Equally did the number seven play a prominent part in the architecture of temples and palaces. The famous pagoda of Churingham is surrounded by seven square walls, painted in seven different colours, and in the middle of each wall is a seven storied pyramid; just as in the antediluvian days the temple of Borsippa, now the Birs-Nimrud, had seven stages, symbolical of the seven concentric cycles of the seven spheres, each built of tiles and metals to correspond with the colour of the ruling planet of the sphere typified.

These are all "remnants of paganism" we are told--traces "of the superstitions of old, which, like the owls and bats in a dark subterranean, flew away to return no more before the glorious light of Christianity"--a statement but too easy of refutation. If the author of the article in question has collected hundreds of instances to show that not only the Christians of old but even the modern Christians have preserved the number seven, and as sacredly as it ever was before, there might be found in reality thousands. To begin with the astronomical and religious calculation of old of the pagan Romans, who divided the week into seven days, and held the seventh day as the most sacred, the Sol or Sunday of Jupiter, and to which all the Christian nations especially the Protestants--make puja to this day. If, perchance, we are answered that it is not from the pagan Romans but from the monotheistic Jews that we have it, then why is not the Saturday or the real "Sabbath" kept instead of the Sunday, or Sol's day?

If in the "Rámáyana" seven yards are mentioned in the residences of the Indian kings; and seven gates generally led to the famous temples and cities of old, then why should the Frieslanders have in the tenth century of the Christian era strictly adhered to the number seven in dividing their provinces, and insisted upon paying seven "pfennigs" of contribution? The Holy Roman and Christian Empire has seven Kurfursts or Electors. The Hungarians emigrated under the leadership of seven dukes and founded seven towns, now called Semigradyá (now Transylvania). If pagan Rome was built on seven hills, Constantinople had seven names--Bysance, Antonia, New Rome, the town of Constantine, The Separator of the World's Parts, The Treasure of Islam, Stamboul--and was also called the city on the seven Hills, and the city of the seven Towers as an adjunct to others. With the Mussulmans "it was besieged seven times and taken after seven weeks by the seventh of the Osman Sultans." In the ideas of the Eastern peoples, the seven planetary spheres are represented by the seven rings worn by the women on seven parts of the body--the head, the neck, the hands, the feet, in the ears, in the nose, around the waist--and these seven rings or circles are presented to this time by the Eastern suitors to their brides; the beauty of the woman consisting in the Persian songs of seven charms.

The seven planets ever remaining at an equal distance from each other, and rotating in the same path, hence, the idea suggested by this motion, of the eternal harmony of the universe. In this connection the number seven became especially sacred with them, and ever preserved its importance with the astrologers. The Pythagoreans considered the figure seven as the image and model of the divine order and harmony in nature. It was the number containing twice the sacred number three or the "triad," to which the "one" or the divine monad was added: 3 + 1 + 3. As the harmony of nature sounds on the key-board of space, between the seven planets, so the harmony of audible sound takes place on a smaller plan within the musical scale of the ever-recurring seven tones. Hence, seven pipes in the syrinx of the god Pan (or Nature), their gradually diminishing proportion of shape representing the distance between the planets and between the latter and the earth--and, the seven-stringed lyre of Apollo. Consisting of a union between the number three (the symbol of the divine triad with all and every people, Christians as well as pagans) and of four (the symbol of the cosmic forces or elements), the number seven points out symbolically to the union of the Deity with the universe; this Pythagorean idea was applied by the Christians--(especially during the Middle Ages)--who largely used the number seven in the symbolism of their sacred architecture. So, for instance, the famous Cathedral of Cologne and the Dominican Church at Regensburg display this number in the smallest architectural details.

No less an importance has this mystical number in the world of intellect and philosophy. Greece had seven sages, the Christian Middle Ages seven free arts (grammar, rhetoric, dialectics, arithmetic, geometry, music, astronomy). The Mahometan Sheikh-ul-Islam calls in for every important meeting seven "ulems." In the Middle Ages an oath had to be taken before seven witnesses, and the one, to whom it was administered, was sprinkled seven times with blood. The processions around the temples went seven times, and the devotees had to kneel seven times before uttering a vow. The Mahometan pilgrims turn round Kaaba seven times, at their arrival. The sacred vessels were made of gold and silver purified seven times. The localities of the old German tribunals were designated by seven trees, under which were placed seven "Schoffers" (judges) who required seven witnesses. The criminal was threatened with a seven-fold punishment and a seven-fold purification was required as a seven-fold reward was promised to the virtuous. Everyone knows the great importance placed in the West on the seventh son of a seventh son. All the mythic personages are generally endowed with seven sons. In Germany, the king and now the emperor cannot refuse to stand as god-father to a seventh son, if he be even a beggar. In the East in making up for a quarrel or signing a treaty of peace, the rulers exchange either seven or forty-nine (7 X 7) presents.

To attempt to cite all the things included in this mystical number would require a library. We will close by quoting but a few more from the region of the demoniacal. According to authorities in those matters--the Christian clergy of old-- a contract with the devil had to contain seven paragraphs, was concluded for seven years and signed by the contractor seven times; all the magical drinks prepared with the help of the enemy of man consisted of seven herbs; that lottery ticket wins, which is drawn out by a seven-year old child. Legendary wars lasted seven years, seven months and seven days; and the combatant heroes number seven, seventy, seven hundred, seven thousand and seventy thousand. The princesses in the fairy tales remained seven years under a spell, and the boots of the famous cat--the Marquis de Carabas--were seven leagued. The ancients divided the human frame into seven parts; the head, the chest, the stomach, two hands and two feet; and man's life was divided into seven periods. A baby begins teething in the seventh month; a child begins to sit after fourteen months (2 X 7); begins to walk after twenty-one months (3 X 7); to speak after twenty-eight months (4 X 7); leaves off sucking after thirty-five months (5 X 7); at fourteen years (2 X 7) he begins to finally form himself; at twenty-one (3 X 7) he ceases growing. The average height of a man, before mankind degenerated, was seven feet; hence the old Western laws ordering the garden walls to be seven feet high. The education of the boys began with the Spartans and the old Persians at the age of seven. And in the Christian religions--with the Roman Catholics and the Greeks--the child is not held responsible for any crime till he is seven, and it is the proper age for him to go to confession.

If the Hindus will think of their Manu and recall what the old Shastras contain, beyond doubt they will find the origin of all this symbolism. Nowhere did the number seven play so prominent a part as with the old Aryas in India. We have but to think of the seven sages--the Sapta Rishis; the Sapta Loka--the seven worlds; the Sapta Pura--the seven holy cities; the Sapta Dvipa--the seven holy islands; the Sapta Samudra--the seven holy seas; the Sapta Parvatta--the seven holy mountains; the Sapta Arania--the seven deserts; the Sapta Vriksha--the seven sacred trees; and so on, to see the probability of the hypothesis. The Aryas never borrowed anything, nor did the Brahmans, who were too proud and exclusive for that. Whence, then, the mystery and sacredness of the number seven?[72]

Chapter 7: The M7th

7:) The I Ching Hexagram Number 7
Stands for "Leading" also "The Army & The Troops"

The Chinese Double Sevens Festival: Zhinu, The Cowherd and Niulang, The Weaver Girl is an Ancient Chinese Mythology Story that is dated to be 2,700 years old. The Cowherd represents the Altair star system located in the Aquila constellation. The Weaver Girl represents the The Brightest star which is Vega located in the Lyra constellation. They also had 2 children who represent B Aquila & Y Aquila The story goes like this: The Jade Emporer in Heaven learned that his daughter The Weaver Girl married a poor cowherd and lived a happy life. The union between Zhinu and Niulang was considered to be forbidden. To ensure their separation the Jade Emperor relocated them to the opposite side of the Silver river. The Silver river represents the Milky way.

Once a year the Magpie birds gather together to form a bridge over the Silver river so Zhinu and Niulang can meet. The Magpie bird is considered to be one of the most intelligent animals in the world. The bird also symbolizes good luck and good fortune. The bridge of Magpies is built over the star Deneb in the Cygnus constellation. This occurs for only a single night, on the seventh night of the seventh moon. Therefore, July 7th is regarded as the Chinese Valentine's Day.

Seven Gods of Luck or Shichi Fukujin: Patrons of good fortune and longevity of Japanese mythology: a syncretism of Shinto and Buddhist concepts, formalized during the 16th century. They are: benten, patroness of the fine arts, female beauty, and a giver of wealth; Bishamonten, also a giver of wealth; Daikoku, god of inexhaustible wealth, usually depicted standing two rice bags and carrying one on his shoulder; Ebisu, god of fishing and food and honest dealing, depicted with a merry face and a fishing rod with which he catches the fish of good luck out of the sea: Fukurokuju, god of fortune and longevity, depicted with the crane, symbol of long life; Hotei, the fat and cheerful god who carries a bag of treasure, from which he gives to non-worriers; Jorojin, patron of health and longevity. [73]

7:) The Seven Gods of Good Fortune Tosa Mitsuoki (Japanese, 1617–1691)

Throughout the ages in every religion the 7 was a symbol of the ensouled, living man. The Pythagoreans called this number "the vehicle of life" since it contained body and soul: 6 applied to the physical dimensions of height and depth, front and back, right and left sides, and is animated by the 7th dimension, the living, vital essence within which is the immortal spirit.

Spiritual man is known to have 7 senses, the 5 physical of sight, touch, smell, taste, and hearing plus the 6th of mental perception and the 7th of spiritual understanding.

The 7 was sacred because it contained 3 and 4: 4 being matter and 3 being the spirit that activates it. The Kabala shows the cube representing matter when it is unfolded and becomes a cross of 4 squares down and 3 across. This is the Tau form that symbolizes the element of life (*The Secret Doctrine*: vol. 2:600).

The 7 was sacred to life because babies who were born in the 7th month generally lived, while those born in the 8th month perished. Pythagoras said this was because 7 is composed of 3 and 4, masculine and feminine number or force and unable to supply the strength needed to survive.

The figure 7 is like the Monad (the number 1) but with a line extending from the head, thus : 7, to depict the event. It also portrays the helmet that Minerva wore. So 7 is representative of helmet shapes, horned shapes, crescent forms, and shapes with curves on the right side. In the law of opposites, 7 is "crooked and straight." Minerva is the Goddess of strategic warfare, and the sponsor of arts, trade, and strategy.

There are 7 creative double letters in the Sepher Yetzirah and there are 7 Elohim who make up the manifested aspects of the Godhead. There's are the same 7. In Christian scripture they are referred to as "the sons of God" and are the ones who say, "Let us make man in *our* image, after *our* likeness…." (Genesis 2:26).

Every culture has reference to these 7 primordial powers which are the Elohim, nature powers, or planetary gods, the creative hierarchies. Their tools are the 7 primary colors and the 7 tones of music that supply the keynote of vibration to every living thing.

Pythagoras calculated the tones of the planets according to their distance from each other, reasoning that their movement creates a vibration which in turn creates a musical sound.

He was led to this enlightenment by observing that the effect of a sound emanating from a vibrating string was controlled by the mathematical proportions, or by the length of the string when plucked.

There were 7 tones. The whole Cosmos is in a state of vibration, the overtones emanating from the fundamental tone of the original Monad, or Creative Deity. These tones compose the "Music of the Spheres" and the "Voices of Nature" (The Sacred Word and Its Creative Overtones: 3).

There were also 7 vowels in the Greek alphabet, 7 basic colors, and 7 metals, and Pythagoras assigned one of each to the 7 planets:

Each planet corresponds to 1 of 7 basic wavelengths. Like music, they have their octaves depending upon their rate of vibration; the slowest is the color red, the musical note C, the planet Mars, the vowel O, and the metal iron. The lower the rate, the more physical, and the higher the rate, the more spiritual.

Pythagoras was known to have taken children with a 7 birth path into his schools of mystery, this birth path meaning they were born to pursue this course.

The 7th Sephira is called Netzach, "Firmness and Victory." For this is where perfection is reached. Through the first six Sephiroth a man can evolve intellectually, but until he responds to his center of spirituality which
Is the light of illumination within, he cannot achieve Victory

The body has six sides. Netzach, 7, is the spiritual center that represents the spark of the deity within every man. It is also the first Sephira that makes up the personality. It has to do with expressing the arts, music, poetry, all which takes creative imagination. In creating things of beauty through the use of the imagination, the person develops his ability as a creator and that is his likeness of God.

Netzach is the right leg of the Adam Kadmon and stands for the instincts and emotions; its opposite and balance called HOD (8) is the left leg and stands for intellect. A proper balance is needed between the 2 because intellect alone is cold and calculating.

Here is the difference between material and spiritual man. Material man is able to gain much through intellect but until there is that inner illumination of the spiritual self, he cannot grow into his full perfection. [74]

Seventh Son: A seventh son is always a lucky or especially gifted person, often gifted with occult powers. He makes a good doctor; he usually has instinctive knowledge of magic and medicinal herbs; and the 7th of a seventh son can stop hemorrhages. Throughout England, Scotland, Ireland, and the United States in general, any 7th child is regarded as having exceptional healing powers. In Ireland, the spittle of a 7th consecutive so is said to be "gifted with the lily" (i.e. fleur de lis). The gift seems to be a kind of clairvoyance or telepathy by which hidden things are brought to light. Among Gipsies, the 7th daughter of a 7th daughter always tells a true fortune. Rumanian folk belief in regard to a 7th child is more sinister: any 7th child is doomed to become a vampire. [75]

7:) Gad, from The Twelve Sons of Jacob
Engraver: Jacques de Gheyn II 1565–1629 The Hague
After: Karel van Mander III, Dutch, 1608-1670
Gad lived from 1564 BCE – 1329 BCE

GAD

By: Emil G. Hirsch, Isaac Broydé, M. Seligsohn, J. Frederic McCurdy

1. The seventh of Jacob's sons, the first-born of Zilpah, himself the father of seven sons (Gen. xxx. 10, 11; xlvi. 16; Num. xxvi. 15 et seq.). The name means "[good] fortune."

2. Biblical Data:

Tribe descended from Gad, the seventh son of Jacob. In the desert it was credited with 40,000 men able to bear arms (Num. i. 24 et seq., ii. 15, xxvi. 18). Rich in flocks, it occupied, with Reuben and half of Manasseh, the district east of the Jordan once belonging to the kings of Heshbon and Bashan and partly settled by Ammonites (Num. xxxii. 1, 29, 33; Deut. iii. 12, 18; Josh. xiii. 25). Hence the "land of Gad" (I Sam. xiii. 7), on the Jabbok (= "brook of Gad"; II Sam. xxiv. 5; see

Gilead). Among its cities were Ramoth, Jaezer, Aroer, Dibon (Num. xxxii. 34 et seq.; Deut. iv. 43; Josh. xx. 8). Gad was a warlike tribe, and took part in the conquest of the trans-Jordanic regions (Gen. xlix. 19; Deut. xxxiii. 20, 21; Num. xxxii. 6 et seq.). Among David's men at Adullam, Gad was well represented (I Chron. xii. 8; I Sam. xxii. 1, 2). Though Gad at first remained loyal to Ish-bosheth, it later transferred its allegiance to David (II Sam. ii. 8 et seq., xvii. 24 et seq.). Jeroboam built the fortress Penuel to keep the men of Gad in check (I Kings xii. 25). Later, under Uzziah and Jotham, Gad was joined to the kingdom of Judah (I Chron. v. 16; comp. Schrader, "K. B." ii. 27). The Ammonitesseem to have ultimately reconquered the territory of Gad (Jer. xlix. 1).

—In Rabbinical Literature:

Gad was born on the tenth of Ḥeshwan, and lived 125 years (Ex. R. i. 5; Yalḳ., Ex. 1). He was called "Gad" after the manna, which was like coriander (; Ex. R. l.c.). Because of his great strength he was not presented by Joseph to Pharaoh, lest the latter should appoint him one of his guards (Gen. R. xcv. 4). Foreseeing that the children of Gad would devote themselves to the breeding of cattle, Jacob ordered that in carrying his bier Gad should walk on the southern side, whence came the beneficent rains and fructifying dew (Num. R. iii. 12). The tribe of Gad occupied the southern side of the camp also (Num. R. l.c.). They were neighbors of Korah because, like him, they were quarrel-some. Their standard was of red and black, with a camp painted on it (Num. R. ii. 6). According to some, the name of Gad was inscribed on the agate in the breastplate of the high priest ("Shalshelet ha-Ḳabbalah," p. 13), according to others on the ligure (Samuel Ẓarẓa, "Meḳor Ḥayyim" to Ex. xxviii.), while others declare it to have been cut on the amethyst, which has the virtue of infusing martial courage (Ex. R. xxxviii.; Baḥya ben Asher's commentary, ad loc.). The tribe of Gad is blamed for having chosen the "other side" of the Jordan, the verse "Riches kept for the owners thereof to their hurt" (Eccl. v. 12) being applied to them (Gen. R. l. 11). When they arrived at the Jordan and saw the fertility of the land, they said: "One handful of enjoyment on this side is better than two on the other" (Lev. R. iii. 1). However, because they crossed the river to help their brethren in the conquest of Palestine, just as Simeon did when he took his sword and warred against the men of Shechem, they were found worthy to follow the tribe of Simeon at the sacrifices on the occasion of the dedication of the Tabernacle (Num. R. xiii. 19). Moses was buried in the territory of Gad (Soṭah 13b; Yalḳuṭ, Wezot ha-Berakah, p. 961). According to some, Elijah was a descendant of Gad (Gen. R. lxxi.). The tribes of Gad and Reuben were the first that went into exile (Lam. R. i. 5).

—Critical View:

The inscription on the Moabite Stone, 1. 10, reports that "the man of Gad had dwelt since days of old in the land of Ataroth; then the King of Israel built for himself Ataroth." According to this, the Moabites distinguished between Gad and Israel, regarding the former as old inhabitants of the parts east of the Jordan. The same notion that Gad is not of pure Israelitish stock underlies the Biblical genealogy of the tribe's eponym. He is the son of Zilpah, Leah's handmaid, not a full brother to Reuben and the other northern tribes. The geographical notes on Gad are for the same reason diverse and divergent. The city of Dibon is designated in Num. xxxiii. 45 as belonging to Gad (with Ataroth and Aroer in Num. xxxii. 34 et seq.), but in Josh. xiii. 15 et seq. this same territory, north of the Arnon, belongs to Reuben. The boundaries of Gad in Josh. xiii. 24-27 (P) are also different. These and other discrepancies show a wide latitude and indefiniteness in the use of "Gad" as a territorial designation. Gilead sometimes includes Gad (among other passages see Judges v. 17), though at times it denotes a country north of Gad, and again a country south of Jaazer (II Sam. xxiv. 5; Josh. xiii. 24 et seq.). These facts seem to indicate that "Gad" was originally the name of a nomadic tribe, and was then applied to the territory which this tribe passed over and settled in. The gradual extension of the use of the name shows on the whole that the tribe coming from the south pushed on steadily northward (II Sam. xxiv. 5; comp. I Chron. v. 11, 16). The territory was never secure from invasion and attacks. To the south it was exposed to the Moabites, to the north to the Arameans from Damascus, and later to the Assyrians. Tiglath-pileser III. annexed this region about 733-732 B.C., and enslaved a part of the inhabitants (II Kings xv. 29; I Chron. v. 26). Ezekiel assigns to Gad the southern boundary in his territorial scheme (Ezek. xlviii. 27, 28). The suggestion has been made that the name of the tribe is derived from Gad, the god of luck.

3. A prophet, "the seer of David." The first appearance of Gad occurred when David took refuge from Saul in a stronghold in Mizpeh of Moab (I Sam. xxii. 5). Gad advised him to leave it for the forest of Hareth. He reappeared late in the life of David, after the latter's numbering of the people, giving him the choice of one of three punishments, one of which God was about to inflict upon the Jews (II Sam. xxiv. 11-14; I Chron. xxi. 9-13). Attached to the royal house, Gad was called "David's seer" (II Sam. xxiv. 11; I Chron. xxi. 9). He also wrote a book of the acts of David (ib. xxix. 29), and assisted in arranging the musical service of the house of God (II Chron. xxix. 25).

4. Name of the god of fortune, found in Isa. lxv. 11, along with Meni, the name of the god of destiny. The passage refers to meals or feasts held by Hebrews in Babylonia in honor of these deities. Nothing is known of any Babylonian divinity of the name of Gad, but Aramean and Arabic equivalents show that the same god was honored among the other leading Semitic peoples. The root-verb means "to cut" or "to divide." Thence comes the idea of portioning out, which is also present in the word "Meni," the name of the kindred deity.

"Gad" is perhaps found also in Gen. xxx. 11, where the ketib reading means "by the help of Gad!" the exclamation of Leah at the birth of Zilpah's son. Indeed, it is quite possible that this narrative arises from a tradition connecting the tribal eponym with the Deity Himself. How wide-spread the cult of Gad, or Fortune, was in the old Canaanitish times may be inferred from the names "Baalgad," a city at the foot of Mount Hermon, and "Migdal-gad," in the territory of Judah. Compare also the proper names "Gaddi" and "Gaddiel" in the tribes of Manasseh and Zebulun (Num. xiii. 10, 11). At the same time it must not be supposed that Gad was always regarded as an independent deity. The name was doubtless originally an appellative, meaning "the power that allots." Hence any of the greater gods supposed to favor men might be thought of as the giver of good fortune and be worshiped under that appellative. It is possible that Jupiter may have been the "Gad" thus honored. Among the Arabs the planet Jupiter was called "the greater Fortune," while Venus was styled "the lesser Fortune." If the same usage prevailed in earlier Semitic days Meni should perhaps also be identified with Venus.

Gad, the god of fortune, is frequently invoked in Talmudic (magic) formulas of good will and wishes; for instance, in Shab. 67b ("Gad eno ella leshon 'abodat kokabim"; comp. Targ. Pseudo-Jonathan to Gen. xx. 10, 11). The name is often synonymous with "luck" (Yer. Ned. iv. 38d; Yer. Shab. xvi. 15d). Gad is the patron saint of a locality, a mountain (Ḥul. 40a), of an idol (Gen. R. lxiv.), a house, or the world (Gen. R. lxxi.). Hence "luck" may also be bad (Eccl. R. vii. 26). A couch or bed for this god of fortune is referred to in Ned. 56a.

Chapter 7
The Holy

The 7's of
The Book of Revelations

The Book of Jude
1: 14 And Enoch also, the 7th from Adam, prophesied of these, saying, Behold, the Lord cometh with 10,000 of his saints.

The Book of Deuteronomy
33:20 And of Gad he said, Blessed be he that enlargeth Gad: he dwelleth as a lion, and teareth the arm with the crown of the head

The 7 Eternals of The Book of Hebrew
5:6: As he saith also in another place, Thou ART A PRIEST FOR EVER AFTER THE ORDER OF MELCHISEDEC (A Priest forever)
5:9 And being made perfect, he became the author of eternal salvation unto all them that obey him; (Eternal Salvation)
6: 2 Of the doctrine of baptisms, and of laying on of hands, and of resurrection of the dead, and of eternal judgment. (Eternal Judgment)

9:12 Neither by the blood of of goats and calves, but by his own blood he entered in once into the holy place, having obtained eternal redemption *for us* (Eternal Redemption)

9:14 How much more shall the blood of Christ, who through the eternal Spirit offered himself without spot to God, purge your conscience from dead works to serve the living God. (Eternal Spirit)

9:15 And for this cause he is the mediator of the new testament, that by means of death, for the redemption of the transgressions *that were* under the first testament, they which are called might receive the promise of eternal inheritance. (Eternal Inheritance)

13:20 Now the God of Peace, that brought again from the dead our Lord Jesus, that great shepherd of the sheep, through the blood of the everlasting covenant. (Eternal Covenant)

Jesus's 7 Statements while on The Cross
The Book of Luke

23:34 "Jesus said, "Father, forgive them, for they do not know what they do. And they parted is raiment, and cast lots.

23:43 And Jesus said unto him, Verily I say unto thee, To day shalt thou be with me in Paradise.

The Book of Matthew

27:46 And about the Ninth hour Jesus cried with a loud voice, saying, Eli, Eli, La-ma, sa-bach- tha-ni? That is to say, MY GOD, MY GOD, WHY HAST THOU FORSAKEN ME?

The Book of John

19:26 When Jesus therefore saw his mother, and the disciple standing by, whom he loved, he saith unto his mother, Woman, behold thy son!

19:28 After this Jesus knowing that all things were now accomplished, that the scripture might be fulfilled, saith, I thirst

19:30 When Jesus therefore had received the vinegar, he said, It is finished: and he bowed his head, and gave up the ghost.

The Book of Luke

23:46 And when Jesus had cried with a loud voice, he said, Father into they hands I Commend My Spirit: and having said thus, he gave up the ghost.

Chapter 1

4. John to the seven churches which are in Asia: Grace be unto you, and peace from him which is, and which was, and which is to come; and from the seven Spirits which are before his throne;

11. Saying, I am Alpha and Omega, the first and the last: and, What thou seest, write in a book, and send it unto the seven churches which are in Asia; unto Ephesus, and unto Smyrna, and unto Pergamos, and unto Thyatira, and unto Sardis, and unto Philadelphia, and unto Laodicea.

16: And he had in his right hand seven stars: and out of his mouth went a sharp two edged sword: and his countenance was as the sun shineth in his strength.

20: The mystery of the seven stars which thou sawest in my right hand, and the seven golden candlesticks. The seven stars are the angels of the seven churches: and the seven candlesticks which thou sawest are the seven churches.

Chapter 2
1: Unto the angel of the church of Ephesus write: These things saith he that holdeth the seven stars in his right hand, who walketh in the midst of the seven golden candlesticks;

Chapter 3
1: And unto the angel of the church in sardis write; These things saith he that hath the seven Spirits of God, and the seven stars; I know thy works, that thou hast a name that thou livest, and art dead.

Chapter 4
5: And out of the throne proceeded lightnings and thunderings and voices: and there were seven lamps of fire burning before the throne, which are the seven Spirits of God.

Chapter 5
1: And I saw in the right hand of him that sat on the throne a book written within and on the backside, sealed with seven seals.

5: And one of the elders saith unto me, Weep not: behold, the Lion of the tribe of Juda, the Root of David, hath prevailed to open the book, and to loose the seven seals thereof.

6: And I beheld, and lo, in the midst of the throne and of the four beasts, and in the midst of the elders, stood a Lamb as if had been slain, having seven horns and seven eyes, which are the seven Spirits of God sent forth into all the earth.

The 7 Seals Explained

Chapter 6
The 1st Seal

1: And I saw when the Lamb opened one of the seals, and I heard, as it were the noise of thunder, 1 of the 4 beasts saying, Come and See.

2: And I saw, and behold a white horse: and he that sat on him had a bow; and a crown was given unto him: and he went forth conquering, and to conquer.

The 2nd Seal

3: And when he had opened the second seal, I heard the second beast say, Come and See.
4: And there went out another horse that was red: and power was given to him that sat thereon to take peace from the earth, and that they should kill one another: and there was given unto him a great sword.

The 3rd Seal

5: And when he has opened the 3rd seal, I heard the 3rd beast say, Come and See. And I beheld, and lo a black horse; and he that say on him had a pair of balances in his hand.
6: And I heard a voice in the midst of the 4 beasts say, A measure of wheat for a penny and 3 measures of barley for a penny; and see thou hurt not the oil and the wine.

The 4th Seal

7: And when he had opened the 4th seal, I heard the voice of the 4th beast say, Come and See.
8. And I looked, and behold a pale horse: and his name that sat on him was Death, and Hell followed with him. And power was given unto them over the 4th part of the Earth, to kill with sword, and with hunger, and with death, and with the beasts of the earth.

The 5th Seal

9: And when he opened the 5th seal, I saw under the altar the souls of them that were slain for the word of God, and for the testimony which they held:
10: And they cried with a loud voice, saying, How long, O Lor, holy and true, dost thou not judge and avenge our blodd on them that dwell on the earth?
11: And white robes were given unto every one of them; and it was said unto them, that they should rest yet for a little season, until their fellowservants also and their brethren, that should be killed as they were, should be fulfilled.

The 6th Seal

12: And I beheld when he had opened the 6th seal, and, lo, there was a great earthquake; and the sun became black as sackcloth of hair, and the moon became as blood;
13: And the stars of heaven fell unto thearth, even as a fig tree casteth her untimely figs, when she is shaken of amighty wind,
14: And And the heaven departed as a scroll when it is rolled together; and every mountain and island were moved out of their places.
15: And the Kings of the earth, and the GreatMen, and the Rich Men, and The Chief Captains, and the Mighty men, and every bondman, and every free man, (7

types of men) hid themselves in the dens and in the rocks of the mountains; (2 locations)

16: And said to the mountains and rocks, Fall on us, and hide us from the face of him that sitteth on the throne, and from the wrath of the Lamb;

17: For the great day of his wrath is come; and who shall be able to stand?

Chapter 7

1.And after these things I saw 4 angels standing on the 4 corners of the Earth, holding the 4 winds of the Earth, that the wind should not blow on the Earth, nor on the sea, nor on any tree.

2. And I saw another angel ascending from the east, having the seal of the living God: and he cried with a loud voice to the 4 angels, to whom it was given to hurt the Earth and the Sea.

3: Saying Hurt not the Earth, neither the sea, nor the trees, till we have sealed the servants of our God in their foreheads.

4: And I heard the number of them which were sealed: and there were sealed an 144,000 of all the tribes of the children of Israel.

5: of The tribe of Juda were sealed 12,000. Of the tribe of Reuben were sealed 12,000. Of the tribe of Gad were sealed 12,000.

6: of the tribe of Aser were sealed 12,000. Of the tribe of Nepthalim were sealed 12,000. Of the tribe of Manasses were sealed 12,000.

7: Of the tribe of Simeon were sealed 12,000. Of the tribe of Levi were sealed 12,000. Of the tribe of Issachar were sealed 12,000.

8: Of the tribe of Zabulon were sealed 12,000. Of the tribe of Joseph were sealed 12,000. Of the tribe of Benjamin were sealed 12,000.

9: After this I beheld, and lo, a great multitude, which no man could number, of all nations, and kindreds, and people, and tongues, stood before the throne, and before the Lamb, clothed with white robes, and palms in their hands;

10: And cried with a loud voice, saying, Salvation to our God which sittech upon the throne, and unto the Lamb.

11 and all the angels stood round about the throne, and about the elders and the 4 beasts, and fell before the throne on their faces, and worshipped God,

12: Saying Amen: Blessing, and glory, and wisdom, and thanksgiving, and honour, and power, and might, be unto our God for ever and ever. Amen

Chapter 8

1. And when he had opened the 7th seal, there was silence in heaven about the space of half an hour.

The 7 Angels & The 7 Trumpets

Chapter 8

2. And I saw the 7 angels which stood before God; and to them were given 7 trumpets.
3: And another angel came and stood at the altar, having a golden censer; and there was given unto him much incense, that he should offer it with the prayers of all saints upon the golden altar which was before the throne.
4. And the smoke of the incense, which came with the prayers of the saints, ascended up before God out of the angels hand.
5. And the angel took the censer, and filled it with fire of the altar, and cast it into the earth: and there were voices, and thunderings, and lightnings, and an earthquake.
6. And the 7 angels which had the 7 trumpets prepared themselves to sound.
7: The first angel sounded, and there followed hail and fire mingled with blood, and they were cast upon the earth: and the third part of trees was burnt up, and all green grass was burnt up.
1180
8: And the second angel sounded, and as it were a great mountain burning with fire was cast into the sea: and the third part of the sea became blood;
9: And the 3rd part of the creatures which were in the sea, and had life, died; and the 3rd part of the ships were destroyed.
10: and the 3rd angel sounded, and there fell a great star from heaven, burning as it were a lamp, and it fell upon the fountains waters;
11: And the name of the star is called Wormwood: and the third part of the waters became Wormwood; and many men died of the waters, because they were made bitter.
12 And the 4th angel sounded, and the 3rd part of the sun was smitten, and the 3rd part of the moon, and the 3rd part of the stars; so as the 3rd part of them was darkened, and the day shone not for a 3rd part of it, and the night likewise.
13 And I beheld, and heard an angel flying through the midst of heaven, saying with a loud voice, Woe, woe, woe, to the inhabiters of the earth by reason of the other voices of the trumpet of 3 angels, which are yet to sound!

7:) The Seventh Angel of the Apocalypse Proclaiming the Reign of the Lord circa

Chapter 9

1. And the 5th angel sounded, and I saw a star fall from heaven unto the earth: and to him was given the key of the bottomless pit.
2. And he opened the bottomless pit; and there arose a smoke out of the pit, as the smoke of a great furnace; and the sun and the air were darkened by reason of the smoke of the pit.
3. And there came out of the smoke locusts upon the earth: and unto them was given power, as the scorpions of the earth have power.
4. And it was commanded them that they should not hurt the grass of the earth, neither any green thing, neither any tree; but only those men which have not the seal of God in their foreheads.
5. And to them it was given that they should not kill them, but that they should be tormented 5 months: and their torment was as the torment of a scorpion, when he striketh a man.
6. And in those days shall men seek death, and shall not find it; and shall desire to die, and death shall flee from them.
7. And the shapes of the locusts were like unto horses prepared unto battle; and on their heads were as it were crowns like gold, and their faces of men
8 And they had hair as the hair of women, and their teeth were as the teeth of lions.
9. And they had breastplates, as it were breastplates of iron; and the sound of their wings was as the sound of chariots of many horses running to battle.
10. and they had tails like unto scorpions, and there were stings in their tails: and their power was to hurt men five months.

11. And they had a king over them, which is the angel of the bottomless pit, whose name in the Hebrew tongue is Abaddon, but in the Greek tongue hath his name Apollyon.
12 One woe is past; and, behold, there come two woes more hereafter.
13. And the 6th angel sounded, and I heard a voice from the 4 Horns of the golden altar which is before God,
14. Saying to the 6th angel which had the trumpet, Loose the 4 angels which are bound in the great river Euphrates

Chapter 10

3. And cried with a loud voice, as when a lion roareth: and when he had cried, 7 thunders uttered their voices.
4. And when the 7 thunders had uttered their voices, I was about to write: and I heard a voice from heaven saying unto me, Seal up those things which the 7 thunders uttered, and write them not.
7: But in the days of the 7th angel, when he shall begin to sound, the mystery of God should be finished, as he hath declared to his servants and prophets.

Chapter 11

15: And the 7th angel sounded; and there were great voices in heaven, saying, THE KINGDOWMS OF THIS WORLD ARE BECOME THE KINGDOMS OF OUR LORD, AND OF HIS CHRIST; AND HE SHALL REIGN FOR EVER AND EVER.

The 7 Plagues

Chapter 15

1: And I saw another sign in heaven, great and marvelous, seven angels having the 7 last plagues; for in them is filled up the wrath of God.
2: And I saw as it were a sea of glass mingled with fire: and them that had gotten the victory over the beast, and over his image, and over his mark, and over the number of his name, stand on the sea of glass, having the harps of God.
3. And they sing the song of Moses the servant of God, and the song of the Lamb, saying, Great and Marvellous are thy works, Lord God Almighty, Just and True are thy ways, thou King of Saints.
4. Who shall not fear thee, O Lord, and Glorify thy name? For thou only art Holy: For all Nations shall come and worship before thee; for thy judgments are made manifest.
5: And after that I looked, and, behold, the temple of the tabernacle of the testimony in heaven was opened:
6: And the 7 angels came out of the temple, having the 7 plagues, clothed in pure and white linen, and having their breasts girded with golden girdles.

7 And one of the 4 beasts gave unto the 7 angels 7 golden vials full of the wrath of God, who liveth forever and ever.
8. And the temple was filled with smoke from the glory of God, and from his power; and no man was able to enter into the temple, till the 7 plagues of the 7 angels were fulfilled.

7:) A Prostituta da Babilônia - Ponto de Vista Cristão: Colored version of the Whore of Babylon illustration from Martin Luther's 1534 translation of the Bible.

The 7 Bowls of Wrath

Chapter 16

1: And I heard a great voice out of the temple saying to the 7 angels, Go your ways, and pour out the vials of the wrath of God upon the earth.
2: And the first went, and poured out his vial upon the earth; and there fell a noisome and grievous sore upon the men which had the mark of the beast, and upon them which worshipped his image.
3: And the second angel poured out his vial upon the sea; and it became as the blood of a dead man: and every living soul died in the sea.
4: And the 3rd angel poured out his vial upon the rivers and fountains of waters; and they became blood.
8: And the 4th angel poured out his vial upon the sun; and power was given unto him to scorch men with fire.
10: And the 5th angel poured out his vial upon the seat of the beast; and his kingdom was full of darkness; and they gnawed their tongues for pain.

12: And the 6th angel poured out his vial upon the great river Euphrates; and the water thereof was dried up, that the way of the kings of the east might be prepared.
17: And the 7th angel poured out his vial into the air; and there came a great voice out of the temple of heaven , from the throne, saying, It is done.
18: And there were voices, and thunders, and lightnings, and there was a great earthquake, such as was not since men were upon the earth, so mighty an earthquake, and so great.
19. And the great city was divided into 3 parts, and the cities of the nations fell: and great Babylon came in remembrance before God, to give unto her the cup of the wine of the fierceness of his wrath.
20: And every island fled away, and the mountains were not found.
21 And there fell upon men a great hail out of heaven, every stone about the weight of a talent: and men blasphemed God because of the plague of the hail; for the plague thereof was exceeding great.

Bibliography

70. The Origins of English Words: A Discursive Dictionary of Indo-European Roots by Joseph T. Shipley The John Hopkins University Press, Baltimore, Maryland 21218 1984
71. The Universal History of Numbers by Georges Ifrah; Pg. 494
72. H.P. Blavatsky Theosophist, June, 1880
73. Funk & Wagnalls Standard Dictionary of Folklore, Mythology & Legend pg.999
74. Behind Numerology: Complete Details on the Hidden Meanings of Letters and Numbers Shirley Blackwell Lawrence: Newcastle Publishing Co. 1989:, North Hollywood, CA Pg 130 – 132
75. Funk & Wagnalls Standard Dictionary of Folklore, Mythology & Legend pg.999
76. The commentaries of Delitzsch and Dillmann on Isa. lxv. 11;
Baethgen, Beiträge zur Semitischen Religionsgesch. pp. 76 et seq.; Lagarde, Gesammelte Abhandlungen, p. 16; idem, Symmicta, i. 87; Pinches, in Hastings, Dict. Bible; Cheyne, in Encyc. Bibl. s.v. Gad.
77. King James Bible 1611

www.ingramcontent.com/pod-product-compliance
Lightning Source LLC
Chambersburg PA
CBHW042305150426
43197CB00001B/25